MW00573322

THE
PERFECT
STORY

THE
PERFECT
STORY

How to Tell Stories That
Inform, Influence, and Inspire

KAREN EBER

HARPER HORIZON

The Perfect Story

Copyright © 2023 by Karen Eber

All rights reserved. No portion of this book may be reproduced, stored in a retrieval system, or transmitted in any form or by any means—electronic, mechanical, photocopy, recording, scanning, or other—except for brief quotations in critical reviews or articles, without the prior written permission of the publisher.

Published by Harper Horizon, an imprint of HarperCollins Focus LLC.

Any internet addresses, phone numbers, or company or product information printed in this book are offered as a resource and are not intended in any way to be or to imply an endorsement by Harper Horizon, nor does Harper Horizon vouch for the existence, content, or services of these sites, phone numbers, companies, or products beyond the life of this book.

ISBN 978-1-4003-3384-4 (eBook)
ISBN 978-1-4003-3383-7 (HC)

Library of Congress Control Number: 2023936158

Printed in the United States of America
23 24 25 26 27 LBC 5 4 3 2 1

For Dean and Madison.
Make your stories perfect.

Contents

PART FOUR: THE OUTCOME–
TELLING A GREAT STORY

PART FIVE: THE TAKEAWAY–LANDING THE IDEA

CHECKLISTS

Don't Eat the Crayons

I have one brown eye and one green eye. When I was five months old, the blue eyes I was born with started to change into the different colors. The medical term for this is *heterochromia*, and it can be starkly noticeable in the right light. People often stop and stare the first time they notice it, their minds trying to process what they're seeing. I've stood face-to-face with many people who freeze, mouths hanging open as their eyes widen, staring at mine.

I have always *loved* my eyes. They make me special. For as long as I can remember, I have been known as "the girl with different-colored eyes." People are more inclined to remember my different-colored eyes than to remember my name. Someone once told me I would never be able to be a spy because my eyes make me too identifiable. They ruin my ability to blend in. I viewed that as a positive; I like that my eyes make me recognizable.

Elementary school began with the annual ritual of drawing a self-portrait. My first few years, I couldn't remember which eye was which. I would ask the person next to me to point to my brown eye. I'd then twist myself to be faceup over the paper and reach behind my head to color the right eye with a brown crayon. No matter how Picasso-like my self-portrait ended up, it was always clear which one was mine. Every back-to-school night, I felt so proud when my parents were always able to pick out my self-portrait.

As I got older, I realized people didn't know how to respond once they noticed my eye color. There was always a reaction, varying from surprise to joy to inquisitiveness. Some viewed my eyes as a problem. An eye doctor once asked me, "Do you want to fix your eye color by wearing one colored contact?" I stared at him, deeply offended, and asked, "Why would I want to do that? Do you ask each of your patients if they want to fix their eye color with colored contacts?" Why would I want to change the very thing that was core to my identity?

By the time I was a teenager, I came to recognize the exact moment when people would recognize my unique eyes. The other person's words would slow and stop mid-sentence. I could see their eyes dart back and forth from my left eye to my right, over and over again. Then I would brace myself for what always came next:

"Hey, did you know you have two different-colored eyes?!"

Sometimes for fun, I would gasp, put my hand on my chest and exclaim "No! Really?!!"

The next comment was typically: "I know a dog/cat like that!"

Thank you?

Followed by: "You know, David Bowie has different-colored eyes."

"Nope, same color. One pupil was enlarged from an accident."

Usually at this point, they would often call other people over. "Hey, come here! You've got to see her eyes!" Followed immediately by, "How did that happen?"

This was the moment that made everything uncomfortable. Everyone would sit in silence, staring at me, looking rapidly from one eye to the other, as if following a tennis ball in a rally. I felt like a sideshow at the circus, expected to perform a trick. I was being viewed as weird and different, instead of wonderfully unique. The relentless barrage of questions would continue: "What color eyes do your parents have? Do you see the same colors out of each eye? Do your eyes give you any special powers?"

I hated these moments. My frustration grew out of the contradiction: I loved my eyes and hated the burden of feeling on display. The whole exchange made me feel depleted and less than. Just as with the eye doctor who wanted to fix my eyes and change my eye color, I was being treated as different and weird for the very thing I loved about myself. I began to dread these interactions and squirm with the way people stared at me. I was no longer a person; I was an attraction, expected to perform.

One day, frustrated after another pelting of questions, I was determined to change the energy and told the following story:

I was born with brown eyes. When I was four, I was coloring in my room one evening. Dinner wasn't going to be for a few more hours, and I was hungry. I dug into a pile of broken, peeled crayons thrown in an old cigar box and pulled out one that was green. I took a small bite and was surprised at how much I liked the taste. So, I kept eating crayon after crayon until each green crayon in the box was gone. When I woke up the next day, my left eye was green.

Then I would be quiet.

Both children and adults would sit stunned for a minute while they tried to figure out if I was telling the truth. This silence was usually followed by sideways looks, arched eyebrows, and a skeptical, "Really?" I would let them off the hook and say, "No, of course I didn't eat crayons." We both would laugh, and some people admitted they weren't sure.

The first time I told the story, I was so surprised at how different the experience felt. It shifted the attention away from me and onto the story. It was less uncomfortable, and I didn't feel depleted. I no longer felt like a circus act being prompted to perform tricks. It created a lighter energy. It allowed me to reclaim my eyes as something that made me feel wonderfully special.

Even more interesting was the difference in the interaction. Instead of stares and scrutiny, I got laughter and smiles. The story often inspired apologies once people realized the silly questions they asked. The conversation always transitioned to a meaningful connection—one I doubt we would have had without the story. The story became something I was known and remembered for, sometimes decades after hearing it. To this day, I still have people comment that they think of me when they see crayons.

My eyes did, in fact, give me a special power: storytelling. They taught me how to use stories to entertain, engage, inform, and even refocus attention. Stories let me influence and inspire behavior, often leaving people changed as a result.

We embrace stories as children before bedtime or around campfires. We entertain friends with them. We even tell them while waiting for meetings to begin. Whether you're climbing the corporate ladder, leading a team, giving a toast, pitching a VC, posting on social media, or selling a product or service, storytelling is a skill you can and should learn. They help you build trust with your audience, create new thinking, become memorable, and influence decision-making. Even with the increase of AI, having the ability to create connection and relate experiences through stories is key. This is the skill that can gain you career growth and success.

Storytelling is a tool I've used throughout my career. Before running my own company, I was a Head of Leadership Development, Culture, and Chief Learning Officer in companies such as General Electric and Deloitte. In each of these roles, I was responsible for developing leaders to create a positive day-to-day culture for employees. I was often in situations where I was trying to gain approval for leadership development programs and technology investments. Very few people had the authority to give the "yes," but many could say "no." Storytelling was the way to connect to people, slow their "no," and even get them to persuade the approvers.

I was the Head of Culture for a General Electric business with 90,000 employees in 150 countries. I leaned into storytelling with the goal of connecting with each person on an individual level. Stories are the original scalable technology, allowing you to deeply touch endless numbers of people at once. Even if an employee never experienced what I described in a story, they were able to consider, *What does this mean for me?* and think about what they might do if they faced a similar circumstance.

Stories also create a ripple effect. Once I walked into a meeting in Paris to find someone I had never met before sharing one of my stories with the room. Another time, someone quoted *me* back to me, without realizing I was the source. I left GE years ago, and I still get emails from employees about how my stories made them think differently.

In my own company, I work with C-suite and leadership teams in Fortune 500 companies to build leaders, teams, and cultures with keynotes, leadership programs, and team retreats. Storytelling is at the heart of each of these.

Whether helping a leadership team strengthen trust and navigate conflict, integrating cultures after a merger, advising C-suite executives on becoming engaging, memorable communicators, or training managers to become empathic leaders, stories decrease defensiveness, expand thinking, and create connection. I often joke I am trying to save the world from boring meetings, one story at a time. Communication and storytelling are core to inspirational and influential leadership.

Leaders are often allergic to storytelling. Many will spend hours creating the perfect set of slides for a meeting, but they don't spend more than five minutes thinking about what they will say. They prepare to talk at the audience, not connect with them. Many of these leaders have said, "I want to give a TED-like talk." What they really mean is that they want to be able to speak without interruption for 15 minutes and be inspiring. They avoid telling stories that would build inspiring ideas and create engagement—the whole point of a TED Talk.

Storytelling is important inside of work and out. Over the years, I've received many panicked calls: People trying to figure out how to position their story for a job interview. Friends that feel the weight of telling a heart-warming story for a eulogy or wedding toast. Entrepreneurs wanting to sell their products. Employees preparing to give a presentation at work. Each wanting to use a story but not knowing where to begin.

A great story can feel effortless to the listener, as if the result of natural talent. Many talk themselves out of telling a story as though they were missing the storyteller gene. When working with people on storytelling, I tell each of them the same things:

1. Storytelling is for everyone. You already tell stories.
2. Practicing is the key to learning and growing as a storyteller. Each time you apply the steps, you gain skill and ease.
3. Great storytelling includes a desired outcome for your audience: something you want them to know, think, feel, or do differently. Creating a toolkit of ideas helps you select the right story for each audience to achieve that outcome.

4. Telling a story isn't the same thing as telling a *great* story.
5. Waiting for the perfect story is futile. Once you learn how to tell stories, you can take the stories you have and *make* them perfect.

My goal is to make storytelling accessible. I believe you can learn to tell great stories for your audience by scientifically hacking the art of storytelling.

A few years ago, I gave a TED Talk called *How your brain responds to stories—and why they're crucial for leaders*. I described how storytelling is an essential communication tool for leaders, particularly when presenting data. The talk centered on the idea that anyone can learn to become a great story-teller. I used stories to demonstrate neuroscience, describe what makes a great story, and explain how to artfully combine storytelling and data. The opening story of the talk introduces Maria and Walt.

Maria walked into the elevator at work, phone in one hand and a stack of folders in the other. She went to press the elevator button when her phone fell out of her hand. It bounced on the floor and slid down the narrow opening between the elevator car and the floor with a *whoosh*.

The phone made a hollow *thud* as it hit the ground three floors below. Maria's hands flew to her face, and she groaned when she realized it wasn't just her phone. It was a phone wallet that held her driver's license, credit cards, and badge. She stood on the elevator threshold; the doors repeatedly closed on her as she pinged her phone from her watch. Stunned to see the phone was still working, she decided to go to the front desk and talk to Ray, the security guard. Hopefully, he would have an easy solution for retrieving it.

As Maria walked up to Ray's desk, she saw him smile widely. Most people brushed past his desk each morning with barely a nod hello, but Maria always stopped to talk. She was one of those people who remembered your birthday, your favorite restaurant, your last vacation, how you take your coffee, and the last movie you watched. Not because she was creepy or nosy; she genuinely cared about people. It was important to her to have each person feel seen and valued.

Ray's smile slowly disappeared as Maria described what had happened. "That's going to be expensive. They have to stop all the elevators in the building to climb down into the shaft and grab your phone. I don't know how much it will cost, but I imagine it will be about $500."

Maria's shoulders sank as she let out a heavy sigh. "Will you get a quote? If it's under $250, do it."

Right then, I happened to be crossing through the lobby and used my badge to help Maria get into her office. The thought of having to replace her driver's license, credit cards, badge, and phone was beginning to overwhelm her. She sank into her chair and put her head on her desk.

Ten minutes later, Ray called her desk phone. "Great news! I was looking at the inspection certificate in the elevator. It turns out the elevator is due for its annual inspection next month. I'm going to call that in today. They'll be able to retrieve your phone as a part of the process, and it won't cost you anything."

Maria's jaw dropped open. "Are you sure?"

"Of course," Ray said. "I'm happy to help to help you."

A few weeks later I was reading an article in the *New York Times* about Walt Bettinger, the CEO of Charles Schwab. He described the biggest lesson of his career, which came during a university final exam.

After maintaining a perfect 4.0 grade point average, he had one last exam in a business class. He spent days preparing and memorizing formulas.

On exam day, the professor handed out a single sheet of paper and told the students to turn it over. Both sides of the paper were blank.

The professor said, "I've taught you everything I can about business in the last ten weeks, but the most important message is this: What is the name of the lady who cleans this building?"

Walt's heart sank.

He had seen her but never asked her name.

He failed the exam. "That had a powerful impact. It was the only test I ever failed, and I got the *B* I deserved. Her name was Dottie, and I didn't know Dottie. I've tried to know every Dottie I've worked with ever since."

Both Walt and Maria want people to feel seen and valued. Giving time and attention to those around you is one of the most powerful things you can do as a leader. It's easy to get caught in day-to-day demands or only give time to people you think can directly help in some way. The best leaders realize everyone is important.

Do you know the Dotties in your life?

This story is vivid and unexpected. You picture yourself standing in an elevator and feel your stomach sink at the thought of your phone falling down the elevator shaft. The tension builds as you wonder what will happen next. In that story, we all become Maria and Walt. You think, *What would I have done? Would Ray have helped me? Would I have known Dottie? Who are the Dotties I need to get to know?*

The story also creates connection. I've received messages from all over the world. People feel inspired to reach out to a stranger after watching a thirteen-minute video. Except to them, I am not a stranger. They approach me with the familiarity of someone they know. They tell me, "My Dottie is named Andrew, and he delivers my mail" or "This made me realize I should meet the Dotties in my life. Thank you."

The story about Walt and Maria is dissected throughout this book to illustrate the storytelling process. Follow its development from a fragment of an idea into a story tested many times before being told on the TED stage. It did not start great. These were two independent ideas that were interesting on their own, but it wasn't obvious that they belonged together. I worked them through the same steps I describe in this book. Just like the director's commentary for a movie, you will get a behind-the-scenes perspective of my storytelling process. Not only will you witness the story's construction, but you can also compare the experience of the story in writing to the one told verbally in the recorded talk on TED.com.

One of the best ways to become a great storyteller is to observe and learn from others. Many chapters of this book end with an interview vignette from different types of storytellers. Interviews include an executive producer at *The Moth*, a founding director of Sundance Institute, an advertising executive, a former Pixar creative director, a television correspondent, a CEO, a physician, an improv comedian, a museum director, a news journalist, the host of the TED Radio Hour Podcast, a neuroscientist, a video game writer, and a data analyst.

While each person has a unique approach and style, they *learned* to become great storytellers. The interviews include what each person might share if you sat next to them at a dinner party. Many describe what they've learned from telling stories in their profession. A few include stories. Some may resonate with you more than others. Imagine what it's like to walk in each of these storyteller's shoes and take away whatever feels meaningful to you. You may never write stories for neuroscience articles or video games, but experiencing different storytellers can inform your approach.

HOW TO USE THIS BOOK

This book teaches where to find stories, how to tell stories, and how to perfect your stories so that you can build ideas, influence decisions, and inspire action. It won't teach you how to write a screenplay or your own novel. But it will take you through a methodology and approach that works whether you're presenting in a meeting, talking to a customer, preparing for a job interview, selling a product, posting on social media, or giving a toast. The approach shared in this book isn't limited to a specific audience or setting. It teaches you how to tell the perfect story in business or life.

This book is structured after a four-part storytelling method: context, conflict, outcome, and takeaway. If you're new to storytelling, read it straight through. It will methodically take you through each step of creating a great story. If you're already a storyteller, read Part One to learn how to further leverage the science behind storytelling, then pick the sections that feel most relevant. Looking to tell a story for a toast, eulogy, or job interview? Jump to *Chapter 7: Do I Have to Tell a Personal Story?* Checklists are included at the end of the book. These lists consolidate the steps in each chapter to quickly help you find story ideas, tell stories with data, and develop and tell a story.

Storytelling is an art that is grounded in science. The next three chapters explore the roles stories play in building ideas and achieving desired outcomes with your audience. They introduce a storytelling process, explain what happens in your brain when you listen to stories, and show you how to hack the art of storytelling.

PART ONE

Hacking the Art of Storytelling

ONE

Storytelling to the Rescue

At the start of my career, I went to one of my first professional dinners. There were eight of us from a few different companies who were exploring working together. As luck would have it, we turned out to be a painfully quiet table of socially awkward introverts. The fact that we were there to talk about business loomed over us and stilted conversation.

Each attempt to get a conversation going fell flat—like a helium balloon slowly sinking to the ground on its last day. We looked enviously at the other tables, lively with discussion and laughter. Awkward silence hung over ours as we sipped drinks and picked at appetizers. Each person focused on their food instead of making eye contact. Eating was easier than talking. If there were a poster for awkward business dinners, this entire table would have been featured.

While I struggled to think of what to say out loud, there was a lively chatter running in my head: *I hate these dinners. They're awkward and unnatural, and I wish I was at home reading a book or organizing my sock drawer by color.*

I'd love to tell you that I told a story to break the discomfort. But at this point in my career, it hadn't occurred to me that I should be telling stories at work. I didn't recognize the human connection and common ground they could create in a business setting. I willed my brain to think of something to talk about and kept coming up blank. Fiddling with my water glass for the seventh time, I kept my eyes down on my napkin.

Just when the tension got to the point of feeling unbearable, our tablemate Aaron cleared his throat. "I'm building a deck on the back of my home," he announced.

Everyone leaned forward and exhaled with relief. Finally, someone was talking! It was not the conversation starter expected at a business dinner, but we were so grateful for the contribution. At this point, reading the potential side effects of a prescription would have been welcome over silence.

"Before we could frame out the deck, I had to relocate a woodpile," he continued.

"So, I'm taking logs off this woodpile and stacking them in a wheelbarrow. Then I wheel that to the edge of the yard to create a new stack. On the third load, I pull a log off the pile and come face-to-face with a raccoon. We're both shocked. I can't tell if he is more afraid of me or me of him. I freeze in place, wondering what he's going to do and if he'll leap at me."

Aaron got up from the table and began acting out their mutual pose of shock, arms up as if they were under arrest, eyes wide and mouth open. He joked that the black mask around the raccoon's eyes added to the irony of the situation.

Aaron described holding this draw for over a minute, both too afraid to move. Yielding first, Aaron slowly stepped backwards, away from the wood-pile. Once he was several feet back, the raccoon scampered off in the opposite direction.

As Aaron told his story, the table came to life. Laughter replaced tension. Silence became energy. Other tables looked over at ours. Each of us peppered Aaron with different questions. Another dinner guest began telling a story about an unexpected animal house guest. The story not only created a shift, but it also created a connection.

We could all picture coming face-to-face with this raccoon, trying to fig-ure out what to do. It wasn't just entertaining; it made Aaron more relatable. The dinner was to talk about a project where Aaron's company would be a potential vendor for my company. I was bracing myself for sales pitches and lobbying. Instead, I got someone willing to be vulnerable for the sole purpose of improving an interaction. He was my hero for removing the awkwardness from the situation.

After that dinner, I always made time to take his calls and connect—something I doubt I would've done had he not told this story. It made him more human, which made me open to talking with him about work. Sharing that personal story helped him gain my trust. He became approachable, someone I could see myself working with. Each time we spoke, it was like talking with a friend.

I've often thought back to that dinner and wondered, *Did Aaron have that story in his back pocket? Was he trying to stop the silence?* Maybe the raccoon story was Aaron's go-to move for awkward business dinners. But I am glad he took the risk of being vulnerable to create connection and try to change the group dynamic. Had we started with a business discussion, we would have rushed through the dinner as quickly as possible. Instead, the story allowed us to relax and enjoy one another's company.

That dinner was the moment I realized how dynamic storytelling could be when used at work. It can make you relatable and create connection. It came to our rescue that night—forming common ground with a group of strangers, even in the most artificial of settings. And the stories did not have to be about work to have a positive impact. A great story beats a boring business discussion every day. If storytelling could make an insufferable dinner enjoyable, there was limitless potential for what it could do in meetings and interactions.

> A great story beats a boring business
> discussion every day.

While there was vulnerability in telling a story, the payoff was rich. Aaron wasn't our manager. But in that moment, he was leading us to a different interaction and conversation—and we were happy to follow him. Stories can establish leaders in unexpected places. Twenty years later, I remember this random story about a surprised raccoon in a woodpile because Aaron told a relatable story—though I've never been face-to-face with a raccoon.

THE ART AND SCIENCE OF STORYTELLING

Stories are such a dynamic way to create an impact. There is an art and a science to storytelling, culminating in common outcomes for both the storyteller and the listener.

1. Storytelling builds ideas and creates shared understanding and connection.

A C-suite team I was working with was stuck in a pattern. Every month, they'd go through the finances and see the same problem: over $100 million in quality issues. They kept debating policies and procedures that should be implemented. The conversation always focused on the solution and not the cause of the problem.

The underlying problem wasn't operational; it was in trust and communications. People within the organization knew there were quality problems but didn't feel comfortable raising issues. They thought they'd be blamed or that more senior leaders would speak up. What was needed weren't more policies. It was a mindset shift to create a safe environment for raising concerns as soon as they were realized.

I joined a team meeting and told the story of NASA. I described the *Apollo 1*, *Challenger*, and *Columbia* disasters where astronauts died. In each after-action review, NASA learned of employees who knew there were problems but were afraid to raise them. Or when concerns were raised, they were downplayed or discouraged. Determined to create a safety culture, they implemented changes for anyone to stop a launch without retaliation.

As the team listened, their defensiveness lowered. Shame was removed as they recognized other companies faced similar challenges. They became more open to exploring why these problems were happening. Instead of their usual debate, they discussed new ways to listen to employees and to each other. The stories created the shift for a different understanding, connection, and conversation.

A great story acts as a roadmap, guiding your audience through information to build an idea, feeling, or inspire action. They act as an open door, inviting people to come through. Stories create understanding by building relatable, recognizable, and reinforcing concepts for the listener.

Stories have desired outcomes for the audience—something we want them to know, think, do, or feel. While your audience may not always agree, the story creates a common understanding, even without firsthand experience. Storytelling transcends the things that divide us; it is the ultimate uniter and connector.

2. We are changed by stories.

Sebastian was a colleague I didn't interact with often. There wasn't a moment or an event that made us avoid each other. With different philosophies and values about work, we didn't often agree. Living and working on separate continents made it easy not to talk—until I was at a work dinner and the only seat open was next to him.

We exchanged polite business dinner conversation for the first few minutes about projects, upcoming work trips, and vacation plans. I asked how he got into the profession of leadership development. Sebastian shared his career journey describing many obstacles—getting laid off and navigating illnesses. The more he told, the more I recognized similarities we shared. My defensive wall began lowering brick by brick. I found myself gaining empathy toward him. The more empathy I felt, the more curious I became. By the end of dinner, we were making plans to work on a project together. To this day, I seek him out for perspective or advice. All because I was changed by his story.

Have you ever watched a movie and felt your eyes well with tears or a lump form in your throat? Maybe you heard the story of the animal rescue organization that saved an abandoned dog with floppy ears and found yourself wanting to donate money to help fund more rescues. Or you heard a colleague share a story, and you felt a bond with them. This was the result of the stories impacting your neurochemicals and your emotions.

Brain chemistry changes when we experience stories. We'll explore in future chapters how you can measure a difference in levels of oxytocin, the bonding hormone, before and after a great story. A great story increases trust and empathy toward the storyteller, often influencing the thoughts, emotions, and actions of the audience.

3. Stories are memorable.

When I was in elementary school, a criminologist came to talk to our class during career day. I listened with fascination while he told a story about solving a crime with a fleck of paint left on a car involved in a hit-and-run. Through that fleck, he was able to determine the make, model, and year of the car that left the scene, resulting in police finding the exact vehicle and driver.

The criminologist described how he often had to testify in court. I sat up straight and asked, "What do you do when you don't have an answer to a question?" I am a rule-following introvert. This situation seemed like peak discomfort—as if the bailiff would arrest him for not having a response.

He smiled and described a time when he couldn't think of an answer. "I took a drink of water to stall time," he said. "I always have water on the stand in case I need to think."

This story has stayed with me for over twenty-five years. Not only did his career fascinate me, but I also learned a simple, new tactic. Each time I have a difficult conversation, I have water nearby. I've even encouraged friends to bring water to job interviews. His story shifted my discomfort to relief, creating a new idea and memory.

| We remember what we feel. |

Stories dynamically engage the senses by lighting up neurons across our brains. The more our senses and emotions are engaged, the more we associate and store memories with them. We remember what we feel. In the book *Actual Minds, Possible Worlds,* psychologist Jerome Bruner shares that thoughtfully embedding a fact within a story increases the chances of recall by 22 percent!

4. Stories reinforce values.

Jake, a CEO of a successful global company, decided to experiment with sending an email every two weeks to all employees. These emails included short stories of recent conversations and interactions with clients. These stories were about 350 words and could be read with minimal scrolling. Each one described a situation, challenge, and result or realization that Jake was taking forward.

These stories were a master class in leadership. Jake shared his mistakes and reflections of what he learned. Curiosity was demonstrated in the client interactions. Praise and recognition were given. Each reinforced what he valued in leaders. These weren't the company values that were displayed on the website. They demonstrated day-to-day leadership behaviors like reflection, continuous learning, and inclusion.

Unprompted, teams began discussing these stories in their meetings and reflecting on what to take forward. Jake ended up creating a storytelling culture. Because he shared stories about the challenges he faced, other leaders did the same. Teams became more comfortable discussing mistakes and lessons learned. After the first few emails, Jake recognized the ripple effect that resulted from each email. He made them a permanent practice, sending them every few weeks for five years.

Stories demonstrate what we value by describing what is encouraged or discouraged. They're a powerful way for leaders to share ideas and bring people along in their thinking to the same understanding.

5. Stories are interactive.

I got an email two weeks after my TED Talk from an audience member. She said, "When you described Maria dropping her phone down the elevator shaft, I nervously reached into my pocket to feel my phone. Even though I knew I was sitting and not moving, the story made me fear I had lost it."

There are two versions of each story. The first is the one told by the storyteller. The second is the interpretation of the story by the audience as they filter it through their own experiences and understanding. Great stories show ideas instead of telling you facts. They invite the listener to have their own experience of the story. Ever notice how you share a story with a friend and they reply with a similar story of their experience? We listen to each story through our experiences, often evoking other stories and memories.

| Great stories show ideas instead of telling you facts. |

"Tell a story!" is thrown around as advice every day. But most people aren't born great storytellers. I wasn't. It's a skill that can be learned, equipping you with a toolbox of stories to tell with ease. There is a process and science to creating a great story for awareness, influencing action, and even making data-informed decisions.

STORYTELLING MODEL

Great stories involve many pieces. There is a methodical process to creating a story with clarity and then layering on meaningful details. Each step allows you to focus on creating that part of your story before moving to the next. The image below shows the steps and model for building a great story.

We begin in the center of the model. *Collect & Select Potential Story Ideas* is an ongoing part of the storytelling process. Once you have an opportunity to tell a story, you move to *Create Audience Persona & Define Outcomes* for your audience. From there, return to the center of the model to *Select Potential Story Ideas* that best helps reinforce your desired outcome. That selected idea is taken through a framework to *Build Story Structure*. Then you layer and *Add Details, Senses, & Emotions. Sequence the Story* allows experimenting with the order the story unfolds. *Apply Five Factory Settings*, which will be introduced in Chapter 2, validates that you have effectively engaged the audience's brain. *Make Everything Earn Its Place* prevents a rambling story. *Test Story* helps identify any necessary tweaks.

Have you ever made pancakes and had to throw the first few away because they didn't turn out right? But by the third or fourth pancake, they're usually perfect. The same may be true of your stories. This model is intentionally a loop. You may take a story through the process multiple times or move back a step or two to tweak the story. Some ideas don't work the way you hoped, and you need to restart the process with a different one. The following chapters take you through each step of the model in detail to create and tell the right story for each audience and setting.

> The brain responds more dynamically
> to storytelling than to information.

While storytelling is an art, it is also grounded in science. The brain responds more dynamically to storytelling than to information. Neuroscience research over the past twenty years has provided great insight into how we understand, store information, and make decisions. In the next two chapters we'll explore this research and learn to leverage the brain to keep our audiences riveted.

┌─────────────── *SUMMARY* ───────────────┐

Storytelling to the Rescue

See the checklists in the back of the book.

- **Storytelling builds ideas and creates shared understanding and connection**. The story acts as a roadmap to guide the audience to a desired outcome.
- **We're changed by stories**. Neurochemicals are released in response to a good story, creating empathy and trust between the audience and storyteller.
- **Stories are memorable**. We store memories and stories with our senses and emotions.
- **Stories reinforce values**. They demonstrate what is encouraged or discouraged.
- **Stories are interactive**. The audience has their own experience of the story based on their own experiences and memories.
- **Great stories often begin as fragments of ideas** that are built out through a methodical process.
- **The storytelling methodology includes advice on how to**:
  - Collect and select potential story ideas (ongoing).
  - Create audience persona and define outcomes.
  - Build the story structure.
  - Add details, engage the senses and emotions.
  - Sequence the story.
  - Apply the Five Factory Settings.
  - Make everything earn a place in the story.

└──┘

Sarah Austin Jenness

Executive Producer at The Moth *and Bestselling Author*

How do *The Moth*'s stories promote listening?

The Moth's mission is to promote the art of storytelling and to honor the diversity and the commonality of the human experience. *The Moth* looks like a twenty-five-year-old storytelling organization, but it's really an arts organization dedicated to promoting and reviving the art of listening.

These stories expand your idea of what is possible, how your life could go, or how the world works. They can break down preconceived notions and make you feel less alone. Listening to stories in community helps to open up a dialogue that perhaps you couldn't find a way into otherwise. Personal stories break open your idea of what is possible.

And it's not just on *Moth* stages. It's storytelling around the world at dinner tables, on the phone, on a rickshaw, on a bus . . . wherever they show up. There is always an impact on the individual telling the story and those who hear it. You never know who will hear your story or what state of mind they will be in when they receive it. The act of storytelling and story listening is incredibly transformational.

How do you work with storytellers?

I am very much a story midwife. It is your story, but sometimes you don't know how you want to structure it yet. You are coming at the story from a particular angle, and I help you find the specifics that will even resonate with strangers. Is this story about you versus you? Is the story centered on your relationship with your sister and how that evolves? Is it about you and your religion? What is the story really about for you at the core?

The same life experience could be told in fifty different ways. When I begin work with a potential new storyteller, I help to unearth all the pieces. I ask, "Well what was your relationship with your mom like before? Pretend I'm next to you when she says that one line you'll never forget. What are you seeing, thinking, smelling, and feeling?" I dig around to excavate the story.

Then comes the exciting and challenging part. This isn't just a series of events. You are bringing us through the experience, almost as if we lived it with you. This is where the transformation happens for the storyteller and the audience.

The stories are like fingerprints. Why can only you tell this story? This, for me, is the most interesting thing to think about. What are the details, elements, and angles that you can tell—so that no one in the world can tell it the same way?

How do you help storytellers work through their vulnerability?

Storytelling is a gift you're giving to the audience. Stories make you human and help people understand and remember you. They give people a glimpse into your heart and what matters to you. Personal stories are alive—and they're a little different each time you tell them.

For storytelling to be effective, you have to tell on yourself a little bit. The "telling on yourself" is the vulnerability. Start with something that maybe isn't your most revealing story and keep working on at it. The audience will reward you with care and kindness and want to hear more.

TWO

What Happens When
You Tell Stories?

I look forward to every Olympics—winter or summer. Not the opening ceremonies, the medal count, or the most popular athletes in each event. Not even
the stories that spotlight the host city. My favorite things are the stories of the
underdogs. Ones of competitors during coverage of things like the biathlon
or rugby sevens—sports I barely knew anything about before I watched the
games.

These stories highlight the challenges the person has faced in their path to
the Olympics. Before I realize it, I'm sucked in. I learn how they dropped out of
school and worked three jobs. I feel anguish over the changes in coaches, taking
loans, passing of loved ones, and overcoming injuries to fulfill their dream of
attending the games. My eyes brim with tears during interviews as their family
members describe pride for the athlete while wiping their eyes.

By the end of the feature, I'm ready to buy a jersey with the athlete's name
and become a certified fan of the sport I just learned about. There is no way I
am missing their event. I'm now on their cheer squad and with them each step
of the way. I pump my fist with joy at their successes and feel crestfallen at the
moments that don't go their way.

And as their games come to an end, I think, *How did they get me* again?
How did these stories make me care about a person and a sport I knew nothing

about? Why did this five-minute story leave me needing to see their performance? Because each of these stories is masterfully told to engage the brain, hook me, and gain my empathy.

THE FIVE FACTORY SETTINGS OF THE BRAIN

While I've always loved the art of storytelling, I'm fascinated by the science. I've spent years studying research by neuroscientists like Dr. Lisa Feldman Barrett at Northeastern University, Dr. Antonio Damasio at the University of Southern California, and Dr. Paul Zak at Claremont Graduate University. Through their research, I've realized there are fundamental ways our brains interact with and process information. Each plays a role in our survival, understanding, communications, and decision-making. Consequently, they also impact how we interact with stories. I call these "The Five Factory Settings of the Brain." Each is infused throughout the storytelling methodology to intentionally engage the brain and inform the development of great stories.

1. The Lazy Brain: Engaging and Focusing the Brain

The brain has one goal: to get you through the day alive and unharmed. When you do, your brain high-fives you and says, *Excellent, do the exact same thing the exact same way tomorrow.* Each time you do something new or different, such as learn a new skill or take up a new sport, your brain is forced to spend calories. Even something as simple as practicing your signature with your non-dominant hand requires attention and focus. Dr. Paul Zak first described the brain as lazy in his 2015 article "Why Inspiring Stories Make Us React: The Neuroscience of Narrative."

Your brain is the stingiest of bankers, wanting to make sure you aren't taking risks that would bankrupt it of calories. It is also a futurist, making predictions about what will happen so you can respond accordingly. Not just for when you face danger. Movements and gestures are predicted—like the way you place your foot when walking downstairs. Step wrong, and you immediately correct while your brain adjusts for future predictions (Feldman Barrett

2021). The first time you went down a flight of stairs, it took several minutes of trial and error. Now you move without conscious thought. Those neural pathways have been strengthened from years of reinforced predictions about your movement. When your brain predicts correctly, it can conserve and bank calories for those experiences that are new or perceived risky.

About 20 percent of our overall calories are used by the brain, the most of any organ. Between 60 to 80 percent of those calories are spent on predictions and making shifts to prepare the body (Feldman Barrett 2018). You know that explosive burst of adrenaline you feel when you see something unexpected out of the corner of your eye, only to realize it is your reflection in the mirror? That's your brain raising your heart rate and dumping cortisol and adrenaline into your body to prepare it to escape a risky situation.

The brain looks for ways to conserve calories and maintain a reserve. It wants to be as lazy as floating in a pool on an inflatable pink watermelon raft while sipping a piña colada. It loves repetition. This is the reason you binge a TV show or movie you've seen before. Your brain often seeks familiarity, comfort, and the opportunity to hoard calories, particularly in times of stress. When watching something new, your brain works to understand and anticipate the plot. Turn on something you have seen before, and your brain already understands what will unfold. The lazy brain stops paying attention to those things that don't engage it. Stories (and speakers!) that ramble, are predictable, emotionally flat, or even hard to relate to can cause the brain to subtly stop paying attention.

A powerful story forces your brain to put the piña colada down and get out of idle mode. Stories that include raising stakes, tension, or unexpected elements force the brain to pay attention and spend calories. Helping the audience see, hear, feel, smell, taste, and experience what the characters encounter dynamically engages the brain and makes the story more memorable.

2. Minding the Gap of Assumptions: Slowing Assumptions, Creating Understanding

How many times have you been watching a movie or reading a book and guessed the outcome? Or you've been in a meeting and already know what the speaker is going to say, so you start to tune out? The brain hates for things to be incomplete and fills in gaps with assumptions. Our evolution and survival have been dependent on the brain's ability to predict and make assumptions that can help us see options, avert a potential disaster, or shift into lazy mode to conserve calories.

As I described Maria's phone falling down the elevator shaft, you may have automatically thought, *I wonder if she got it back? What would I have done?* Without you consciously willing the thought process, your brain tried to figure out what happened and what *you* might do in that situation.

Our understanding is formed through assumptions we make based on our knowledge and experiences—which may or may not be accurate. You may have experienced this when a friend gave you a weird look. You convinced yourself he was mad at you, only to find out he was trying to remember if he left his car windows down.

A great story helps connect people to a desired outcome that informs thinking, influences behavior, or inspires action. Stories can either slow down or leverage assumptions. Unexpected plot points and the "I didn't see that coming!" moments disrupt assumptions and force the brain out of lazy mode. The same is true when you build tension and highlight what is at stake in a story.

3. The Library of Files: Processing and Categorizing Information

The brain has a massive, connected network of neurons that help process information detected through your senses. We used to think of these neurons as having specific jobs (e.g., vision, taste, or sound); however, there aren't boundaries between senses (Feldman Barrett 2022). Most neurons can carry information for multiple senses along neural pathways. These neurons fire constantly as the brain makes predictions.

When inputs for our senses are detected, they get relayed to respective sensory regions for processing. If a potential threat is detected, the body releases adrenaline and cortisol to increase focus and prepare you to escape danger.

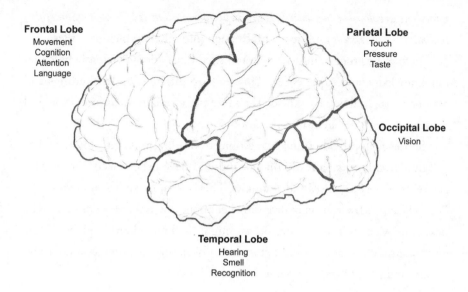

Frontal Lobe
Movement
Cognition
Attention
Language

Parietal Lobe
Touch
Pressure
Taste

Occipital Lobe
Vision

Temporal Lobe
Hearing
Smell
Recognition

Sensory experiences are stamped with emotions and prepared as memories—just as your phone tags photos with camera settings, date, time, and location. These are organized and filed as long-term memories. Your brain refers to these memories, experiences, and emotions to predict how to respond in the future, which has played a pivotal role in humanity's evolution and survival (Feldman Barrett 2018).

Our senses play an integral role in how we experience, tag, file, and recall information. Ever wonder why the smell of fresh cut grass makes you think of running barefoot as a child? Because the sense of smell holds our strongest relationship with memory. We have four different receptors for touch, three for vision—and over 1,000 for smell (Hamer 2019).

Our senses connect emotions with memories. My friend Kathryn was in a car accident as a child where takeout food was scattered all over the car and onto her clothing. Twenty years later, she was in another car accident. She immediately smelled coleslaw when there was none in the car. Senses dynamically engage your brain and its library of files of experiences, knowledge, memory, and emotions.

Your brain processes over thirty-four gigabytes of information through your senses each day, often subconsciously (Bohn 2009). This information is compared with what you already know and understand. Your brain considers, *Is this something previously experienced? Is this new information? Is it related to something previously experienced?* and stores information into different memory "files."

Each of us process, understand, and file information differently based on our knowledge and experiences. This leads to different understandings and assumptions. Individuals can see the same piece of data or information and come away with different interpretations.

Stories help provide filing suggestions to our brains. Great stories anchor to familiar things we already understand and have experienced. Stories also actively engage our senses and emotions. This is what makes them memorable. We feel Maria's frustration of dropping her phone down the elevator shaft. The next time we step into an elevator, we might hold our phones tighter. While everyone may not agree with a story or information, it provides a common understanding and starting point for discussions.

4. Inside the Circle of Trust: Creating Connection and Empathy

With the brain's priority to survive the day, we want to surround ourselves with others who can help make that possible. A group of people can keenly sense danger, protect one another, and accomplish more in a shorter time. These "in-groups" are how humans have survived and evolved.

We naturally form these groups with people with whom we identify, connect, and share similarities. In-groups create a sense of belonging. Out-groups make us feel different or identify as an outsider (Agarwal 2020). Everyone who works at the same company is part of an in-group. But within the company, people who work in HR and Engineering are out-groups from each other because of the differences in their work. We make assumptions and process information differently based on whether we feel a part of a group or not.

> Stories create in-groups when they relate to the audience's "I want that!" feeling.

We feel a part of in-groups when we hear stories that share beliefs, experiences, or aspirations with our own. Empathy and connection are experienced, increasing oxytocin and trust. This belonging helps us feel comfortable, relaxed, or excited. Stories create in-groups when they relate to the audience's "I want that!" feeling.

Stories that create out-groups help you recognize your contrasting experience or perspective. When we feel outside of a group, we often experience heightened awareness, discomfort, and feel different. A charity telling the story of people in Ethiopia without access to clean water helps the audience recognize how different their lives are with indoor plumbing. These stories leverage the natural comparison of circumstances to recognize differences or new ideas. Like in-groups, out-groups often lead to increased empathy and support, spurring action that is motivated by recognition of differences. A company undergoing a merger or embracing a new strategy might tell stories that describe the new direction and why the group can't stay in the status quo.

Great stories are intentionally designed to help the audience feel a part of an in-group or out-group and sometimes both. You may have never dropped a phone down an elevator shaft, but you can see how easily it could happen to you. In-groups and out-groups help the audience connect to the story and the desired outcomes.

5. Seek Pleasure, Avoid Pain: Neurochemicals Amplify the Experience

The neurochemicals in our brain often drive us to do two things: seek pleasure (and sometimes in abundance) or avoid pain and danger (Thomson 2021). Dopamine, endorphins, and serotonin are released in moments of connection or attraction. Oxytocin is released when we feel a sense of bonding and trust toward someone. They each make us feel great and reinforce the pursuit of pleasure and connection. Cortisol and adrenaline are released to increase attention or focus. This prepares us to avoid pain or discomfort and get out of danger when a threat is detected.

Discomfort doesn't have to mean dangerous or negative things. Riding a rollercoaster, watching a horror movie, giving a presentation, learning a language, or bungee jumping can create heightened stimulation. Your body is on alert in the moments you're outside your comfort zone. The experience is amplified with the neurochemical cocktail and range of emotions.

A great story is intentional about how it connects the audience to pleasure or discomfort. We feel Walt's discomfort in not knowing Dottie's name. We also feel Maria's surprise in learning she can get her phone back for free. Connecting the audience to moments of pleasure or discomfort engages them in the story and helps them experience emotions that impact their actions.

Storytelling is a musical conductor of neurochemicals. A great story can create a crescendo of pleasure neurochemicals. It can also amplify the feeling of discomfort or decrease and quiet it to avoid pain. These directly impact how we process information and make decisions. Stories that include uncomfortable moments help you consider what you can do to navigate or avoid them. Those that leave you in a wave of joy and warmth can reinforce the choices, actions, and values in the story.

WHAT HAPPENS IN OUR BRAINS WHEN WE LISTEN TO INFORMATION VERSUS STORIES?

If you were sitting in a coffee shop, you would hear plates and glasses clinking. Chairs scrape on the floor while the espresso machine hisses and bubbles before dripping into a cup. Murmuring conversations float over your shoulder from the other customers. Each bite of a croissant makes a satisfying crunch through the flaky layers. Your brain would recognize and process these sounds at a subconscious level, without you remembering them a few seconds later.

Replace coffee shop sounds with music, and you move from processing and forgetting the noise to dynamically interacting with and remembering it. Whether listening to a Mozart sonata or "Imagine" by John Lennon, your brain lights up with more neural activity than when you're just processing sounds. You notice the melody or harmony. You might tap your toes, and even hum it for the rest of the day. The difference in how your brain processes noise and music is analogous to what happens when your brain processes information and stories.

Wernicke's area is a walnut-sized part of your brain involved with processing language and information. It creates comprehension by decoding words into meaning. As we read or hear words, they're compared to our internal dictionary for understanding.

This area is active when you're reading, sitting in a lecture, or listening to data or details in a meeting. Words are processed and understood; however, only this small part of your brain is engaged. Psychologist Harmann Ebbinghaus found that almost 50 percent of information is forgotten within an hour when you don't interact with it.

When you listen to a story, your brain dynamically lights up. As I described the sounds in a coffee shop earlier, the neurons near your temporal lobe began to light up as though you were hearing the hiss and sputter of the espresso machine. As I further describe the wooden chairs, the wall of bright yellow mugs, and the tie-dyed apron of the barista, your occipital lobe neurons begin to light up as you visualize these items. You may even imagine the rich smell of pastries and coffee, causing activity in your temporal lobe. As you imagine the taste of the coffee and the feel and weight of the mug in your hand, your parietal lobe lights up. Your frontal lobe lights up with movement as I describe the barista swaying in place while pouring coffee.

Stories meaningfully engage each of your senses and create activity across your brain. The sights, sounds, smells, textures, tastes, and emotions show neural activity across each lobe. We know from the third factory setting—the library of files, these senses are often stamped with memories and emotions as they stored. Particularly smell—a whiff of perfume can easily take you back to a special afternoon with your grandmother.

Each time I enter the lobby of any W Hotel, I remember having my hair washed in the kitchen sink when I was four. Whatever fragrance they use in their lobby reminds me of the smell of that shampoo, triggering many wonderful memories. Stories that engage our senses take up more real estate in the brain and put us front and center in the story as though we were experiencing it firsthand.

STORYTELLING: THE ARTIFICIAL REALITY EXPERIENCE FOR YOUR BRAIN

I've been attacked by a shark while swimming in the ocean. I was swimming along the surface when out of nowhere, I was nudged from underneath. The first nudge took me by surprise and started my heart racing. The second nudge felt much rougher, and I realized I was shark bait. I started thrashing on the water, desperately trying to get to shore and safety.

OK, I haven't *literally* been attacked by a shark. But my brain told me otherwise as I watched *Jaws*. Each lobe in my brain lit up as though I were the swimmer on screen. Adrenaline dumped into my body, and my brain yelled, *"Swim!"* while I watched the actor do the same. I could feel myself bobbing in the water with the ocean currents swirling around me. I've even lifted my feet as though a shark were going to come out of the carpet and nip at them.

While I have never been attacked by a shark in the ocean, my brain lets me imagine what it is like when watching the movie. While I sit calmly on my couch, my brain lights up, and my heart begins to race just as though I am the actor onscreen. My senses get activated, and I can imagine the experience. So much so that my brain sends me reminder warnings: *"Watch out for sharks!"* whether I am swimming in the ocean or a pool. Stories create this artificial reality experience for the brain.

Dr. Uri Hasson is a neuroscientist at Princeton who conducted experiments on the similarities and differences in neural activity between communicators and listeners. One experiment had participants watching episodes from a BBC television series while in an fMRI machine that measured their brain activity. They returned to the fMRI a second time to describe the episode from memory. These recounted descriptions were recorded. A different set of participants listened to these recordings while their brain activity was also measured in an fMRI machine.

Hasson found similar brain activity across the three different instances. It didn't matter if participants were listening to or describing the episode. He's replicated this research with different shows and movies. Each time yielded the same result: synchronization in the brain activity of the storyteller and listener.

This *neural coupling* is one of the strongest attributes of storytelling. When listening to a story, a listener's brain lights up and mirrors the same patterns as the storyteller's, particularly when the story engages the senses and emotions. These are the moments you feel a lump form in your throat as you watch a sad movie. Neural coupling is one of the greatest empathy builders—the original artificial reality. The more the listener's senses and emotions are engaged, the stronger the experience.

Want to help people experience something they've never encountered before? Tell them a story. Their brain will engage as though they are the main character. Paris Brain Institute researched the heart rates of participants while listening to stories. They found the listener's heart rate synchronized with the storyteller's. The more engaged the person was in the story, the stronger likelihood that their heartbeats would synchronize. It didn't matter if participants listened to the stories in different cities or at different times from the storyteller. As their brains engaged with the story, the heartbeats would synchronize.

The Five Factory Settings of the Brain not only describe why storytelling is compelling, but they also provide a guide for what makes a great story. The way you navigate and leverage them in your stories directly impacts the experience and engagement for the audience. While you may not engage each of the five in every story, considering them helps to ensure you're telling great stories. Future chapters provide considerations for engaging them throughout the storytelling model.

We tell stories for a reason and a desired outcome. The way these stories are told impacts the experience and outcome for the audience. Mastering the art of storytelling includes understanding the science of how we make decisions. The next chapter explores how to do exactly that.

SUMMARY

What Happens When You Tell Stories?

See the checklists in the back of the book.

Our brains have Five Factory Settings that impact how we engage with and interpret information—especially stories.

1. **Lazy Brain:** The brain is lazy, wanting to conserve calories to keep you alive each day. Great stories force the brain to spend calories by engaging the senses and creating tension.
2. **Assumptions:** The brain continually makes predictions and assumptions based on past experiences. Great stories slow down or harness assumptions with conflict and unexpected events.
3. **Library of Files:** We process thirty-four gigabytes of information into a library of files of experiences, memories, and emotions that are called upon for predictions. Great stories connect to what we already know through specific details and metaphors.
4. **In-/Out-groups:** Stories help us feel part of in-groups or out-groups. In-groups create a sense of familiarity, comfort, and belonging. Out-groups help illustrate the differences of individuals or experiences.
5. **Seek Pleasure, Avoid Pain:** Our neurochemicals help us to seek pleasure or avoid discomfort. In storytelling, this is experienced as stories that make you feel good or uncomfortable.

As we listen to stories, our brains light up in the same patterns as the storytellers. This neural coupling helps us feel like we are in the story, creating an artificial reality experience for your brain.

Michelle Satter

Sundance Institute Founding Senior Director, Artist Programs

What do you look for in a story?

I am looking for an author's truth in how they tell a story—someone's deeply personal perspective and unique voice. Additionally, I respond to how they've created a world and a consistent tone with specificity and detail. I want to invest in the characters who speak and behave from a truthful place, have complexity, and are on an emotional journey with a clear want and need.

I'm interested in discovery—when my heart and mind open up and I feel like I am in the presence of a writer who is going to share their story, vulnerabilities, and unique perspective. It's what I hope for when I open up a book or script.

How do you encourage writers to find their voice?

I feel like everyone has a voice, perspective, and experience of reality, defined by their belief system. You want your audience to be engaged, awake, and invested in the characters and what happens next. Don't think, *What does the market need?* or *What do people want from me?* Think, *What can I give to the world? What is the story only I can tell? What can I bring and communicate to an audience? How will I engage them and surprise them?*

Characters evolve stories. Set your characters on an emotional journey with stakes that build and a structure where every scene moves the story forward or reveals something new about your characters.

How do you approach feedback with writers?

I start by listening and asking questions to learn intentions and what they are hoping to communicate through their story. One important question is, "What is the story about?" Some writers might not know until they've created the work and they look back.

Other questions include, "What's your personal connection to the story you are telling? How do you step into your characters? What is the world you are trying to create? What are the images and sounds in that world?"

It is important to listen to feedback but to not take it personally. Embrace confusion as part of the process that often leads to meaningful discoveries. Ask the hard questions of yourself and of your characters. The right questions can lead you to the most imaginative and surprising solutions.

What advice would you give to the average person telling stories?

Storytelling is essential communication that we all have the ability to do. It has an impact on everything we do. Start by journaling and observing. Write every day. Have awareness and curiosity about the world around you and the behavior and humanity of people. Read scripts, watch movies, listen to how writers talk about their creative process. Be engaged. I've learned from everyone. I feel like my life is a journey of giving, receiving, and learning.

Find a story you are passionate about telling. Writing takes time. It is rewriting. You don't get it on the first try. It's a process of researching, exploring, and trying new ideas with a commitment to the spine of a story, the themes, and what you want the audience to take away. I do believe storytelling has the power to change the world.

Believe in your work. Believe in your voice. We all have something to say that's meaningful that can shape the way we see ourselves, each other, and the world around us.

THREE

Creating Desired Outcomes

A yellow lab puppy digs under a white wooden fence that runs the length of a long dirt road. He wriggles his body underneath it. Once free on the other side, he runs across a field and scampers into a red barn. The puppy's ears flop as he comes to a sudden halt in front of a stall door.

A tall brown Clydesdale with a white splotch on its forehead bends down. The two buddies nuzzle their noses. Across the barn, a door slides open with a thud. The farm owner laughs, picks up the puppy and carries him back to the home next door with a "Puppy Adoption" sign out front. Handing the puppy to the homeowner, they both shake their heads. This isn't the first time this has happened.

The puppy is at the fence again, squeezing his way underneath. He crawls through mud, runs in the rain, and rolls in the grass to visit and play with his friend. Each time, the farm owner treks across the well-worn path to return the puppy to his home.

One day the puppy is scooped up and placed in the backseat of a car. He climbs up into the back window, yelping and pawing at the glass. The Clydesdale stomps the ground, nickers, and gallops toward the car, jumping over fences. Other Clydesdales join the thundering chase. The pack surrounds the car, forcing it to a halt.

The freed puppy leads the trotting Clydesdales back up the dirt road to the farm. Friends reunited, the puppy and Clydesdale play in the grass together.

As the scene fades to black, the Budweiser logo displays with #BestBuds underneath.

This "Puppy Love" commercial premiered during the Super Bowl in 2014 and was quickly a fan favorite. It won awards from *USA TODAY*'s Ad Meter and even received two Emmy nominations. It's memorable, melted hearts, and has racked up millions of views online. Yet, the commercial was a failure. It didn't create engagement in the brains of the audience that led to follow-through sales.

As soon as the puppy runs up to the Clydesdale, the first three Factory Settings of the Brain work in combination. The brain assumes, *"I know what this story is about. The puppy and the horse are friends. They will be separated and must find a way back to each other."* That assumption is made based on the existing knowledge and emotions stored in the library of files in the brain. With the assumptions made, the brain slides into lazy mode to conserve calories, all within the first few seconds.

The commercial is memorable and includes details that trigger your emotions. Who doesn't love puppies or Clydesdales? Watching the two friends frolic releases dopamine and makes us feel good. It's familiar and memorable because of the emotions we feel for both things. But because it is predictable, we don't feel enough tension building. It doesn't frame a new idea or help us think differently. Our brains aren't left at a cliffhanger the way movie trailers try to entice us to stream or buy a ticket. The commercial doesn't inspire making a choice or action—the product isn't even featured. It would be an excellent, calming bedtime story for kids.

Tension is built through conflict and raising stakes—something not experienced until the halfway point when the puppy is put in the car. Starting the commercial with the Clydesdales chasing after the car and revealing the friendship through flashbacks would have immersed us immediately. Or the puppy could have been taken away by the car and later reunited with the Clydesdale in an unexpected way. As it was told, the story had a predictable and somewhat flat arc.

The commercial is well-liked and won awards. However, it did not translate to sales—the desired outcome for an expensive Super Bowl commercial.

Budweiser stopped the puppy commercials once they recognized the lack of follow-through sales.

It's not enough to tell a story. The *way* you tell the story makes a difference in how people connect and engage with it. Each time we tell a story, we have a desired outcome: we want people to know, think, feel, or do something different after. Even when we tell stories with friends, we hope to entertain them or make them laugh. The Budweiser commercial is a great example that there can be a disconnect between what we think we like and what our brains truly engage with when making decisions.

STORYTELLING: THE GREAT EMPATHY AND TRUST BUILDER

Have you ever participated in a meeting, an off-site retreat, or a conversation where you came away feeling closer and more bonded to a person—or even the entire team? You shared stories about hobbies, weekend adventures, life experiences, and vacations over coffee and meals. You gained a more well-rounded understanding of who they were. Your interactions shifted positively as you came away feeling increased trust and empathy toward one another.

This wasn't luck. As you listen to stories, you gain empathy for the storyteller, particularly when sensing their vulnerability. As empathy increases, so does trust. This creates more oxytocin to be released in your brain. Sometimes referred to as "the love hormone" or "the trust hormone," oxytocin impacts bonding behavior—from mothers and babies to social interactions. Oxytocin indicates to our brain who is safe to know and be around, and who should be avoided (Zak 2015). It gives us the nudge to feel part of an "in-group" when we feel a sense of connection and belonging.

Oxytocin is released in response to a stimulus, like a story. It can't be commanded, willed, or controlled. Stress inhibits the creation of oxytocin, slowing the development of connection, trust, and empathy.

Stories compound empathy, oxytocin, and trust, making them an important tool in business and for leaders. The very act of telling a great story will elicit an increase in empathy and trust from the audience. Storytelling cuts through stress and noise, leaving you mentally, physically, and emotionally changed. And on top of *that*, stories also impact the way we make decisions.

Data doesn't change behavior; emotions do.

Do you have a favorite fact or data point? If you can recall one, it's likely wrapped in a story. No one says, "I wish there were more data, charts, and figures in that presentation." Yet there's this firmly held belief that data is what changes our behavior. If data changed our behavior, we would all sleep eight hours, drink eight glasses of water, and exercise and floss daily.

As we consume data, we question its trustworthiness. When someone is presenting data, the listener is working through thoughts like, *Do I trust this data? Do I trust the speaker?* Think of controversial topics where you have deep beliefs—like politics. When you hear someone with an opposing belief share a statistic, you don't often trust it or the person sharing it. Assumptions are made on how the data was manipulated to support the narrative. The heart of decision-making lies in emotions, not logic.

THE HEART AND MIND OF DECISION MAKING

It's tempting to think we make decisions based on facts, data, and logic. However, neuroscience research validates that we make decisions through our emotions. Neurologist Dr. Antonio Damasio studied patients with damage to the prefrontal cortex of their brain. You would never know they had isolated brain damage. They could walk, talk, eat, think, and hold down professional jobs. They had once been vibrant and expressive people. Now, they were emotionally flat. When shown disturbing images of accidents, injuries, or fires, they felt nothing and showed no neurological response.

Their inability to experience emotions also impacted their ability to make even simple decisions. While it might take you two seconds to decide if you should organize your computer files by date or name, they would be rendered stuck and unable to decide.

Damasio and his colleagues conducted experiments to better understand the relationship between decision-making and emotions. In the Iowa Gambling Task experiment, participants were shown four decks of cards, labeled A, B, C, and D. Participants selected one card at a time that could either win or lose money. Their goal was to win as much money as possible. What participants didn't know is that two of the decks were "bad," resulting in higher penalties. Two were "good," resulting in long-term rewards. They were hooked up to telemetry instruments that measured stress reactions, like perspiration and heart rate changes, to capture the moment their brains identified the "bad" deck.

The participants without brain damage were able to recognize and stick with the "good" decks after about forty to fifty selections. The telemetry instruments detected stress responses after ten selections, when their brain subconsciously sensed something was wrong. It took another thirty to forty selections for the participants to become conscious of the "bad" decks.

Participants with the brain damage never detected the "bad" deck—consciously or subconsciously. Their telemetry instruments never detected a physical or stress reaction. Their inability to experience emotions directly impacted their decisions.

In his book *Descartes' Error*, Damasio said, "Emotions and feelings are not a luxury, they are a means of communicating our states of mind to others. They are also a way of guiding our own judgments and decisions. Emotions bring the body into the loop of reason."

Damasio first identified this physical or stress response as the "Somatic Marker Hypothesis" in 1994. It suggests that emotions can impact decision-making by creating a biomarker. Things like nausea, anxiety, sweating, rapid heartbeat, or even a gut feeling are often signals of emotions and memories. When we face decisions, we are guided by our previous experiences and emotions, often unconsciously. Take away the ability to experience emotions, and you take away the ability to make the most basic of decisions.

Researchers from a group led by Professor John-Dylan Haynes in Berlin conducted a similar experiment to identify the moment our brains become conscious of decisions. Participants were placed in an fMRI machine with buttons in both hands representing different choices. Participants were asked to press either button to indicate their decision and verbalize the moment they recognized making the decision. Neurons could be seen traveling in the direction of the choice seven seconds before the person expressed awareness or pressed the button. The choices were made subconsciously before the participants became aware of them.

You too make choices at a subconscious level. At the point you become aware, you apply rationalization and logic. It's like buying a car because you love the color but justifying it because of the gas mileage. You think you're making rationally based decisions, not realizing they were already subconsciously made.

> Stories help us tap into our emotions
> and aid in decision-making.

Emotions are at the heart of decisions, even when you think you're making logical decisions. There is a bias that emotional decisions are bad and rational decisions are good. However, they aren't separate. Emotions and reasoning are intertwined. Stories help us tap into our emotions and aid in decision-making.

THE WAY YOU TELL THE STORY MATTERS

Dr. Paul Zak is a neuroscientist, founder of Immersion Neuroscience, and Professor at Claremont Graduate University. He and his lab combine neuroscience with psychology and economics to understand how people process information and make decisions, especially those involving money. And to me, Dr. Zak is changing the future of storytelling. He and his lab were the first to identify that humans release oxytocin in response to feeling trust toward another person. They measured the impact of telling a story on oxytocin levels. And they've built on that research to get real-time measures of what makes an engaging and immersive story.

Dr. Zak has traveled the world studying the changes in oxytocin based on connection. By drawing blood before and after emotional events like weddings, ceremonies, and interactions, he could study changes in oxytocin levels. He has even traveled to Papua New Guinea, conducting research with indigenous peoples, which he spoke about in his TED Talk in 2011.

As he started to identify the relationship between connection, trust, and oxytocin, Dr. Zak and his lab conducted experiments to see if the use of stories would impact the oxytocin response. They ran a variety of experiments that drew participants' blood before and after listening to a story. The experiments varied the stories in their detail and tension. While the purpose and focus of each experiment differed, the findings were consistent.

One group of participants watched a video of Ben, a young boy playing. His father says to the camera that Ben is two years old and dying of a brain tumor. The father describes his struggle between wanting to be present and happy for his son and knowing he will soon die. While participants watched, they developed empathy for the boy and his father. Their oxytocin levels spiked, and attention stayed high throughout the story. The majority even voluntarily donated a portion of their earnings to a childhood cancer charity.

A different group of participants watched a different video of Ben and his father. This video didn't mention Ben is dying of cancer. His father calls him a "miracle boy." They spend the day at the zoo, wandering around looking at animals. The plot was intentionally flat, making it unclear why you're watching this father and son. This audience failed to empathize with the characters and their attention drifted off midway through. There was no tension or emotion to keep them interested. As a result, there was no elevation in their oxytocin or voluntary charitable donations.

After twenty years of study, Dr. Zak and his team worked out how to predict behavior based on measuring individual brain responses. They developed software called Immersion so that anyone could measure neurologic immersion of stories in real-time without drawing blood. Immersion captures the attention response due to dopamine and the emotional connection due to the release of oxytocin. Applying algorithms to data pulled from smart watches or fitness trackers, the platform captures second-to-second measurement of how immersed or engaged the brain is with a story, information, or even music. The software captures the subtle changes in every heartbeat to infer brain activity.

Dips in immersion can be pinpointed to specific moments. These measurements accurately predict the behavior response of the audience.

The Immersion software has been used to measure audience engagement with commercials, movie trailers, marketing materials, communications, training, speeches, customer experiences—and, of course, stories. It can predict how someone will respond with over 80 percent accuracy. This means a commercial can be tested to predict if it will result in expected sales—or not. This is exactly what happened when Dr. Zak's team ran an independent experiment with a group of volunteers watching Budweiser's "Puppy Love" commercial for the first time.

With wearable devices on their arm, participants said they liked the "Puppy Love" commercial, but the measurement indicated their brains weren't captivated (Zak 2015). Out of all the Super Bowl commercials Dr. Zak's team tested with participants that day, "Puppy Love" ranked at the bottom in the likelihood to convert to sales. The story was too predictable. The participants experienced the lazy brain. Dr. Zak and his team recognized the commercial wasn't effective and predicted it wouldn't result in sales well before Budweiser stopped the campaign.

The Immersion software eliminates the disconnect between what we *think* we feel and our real-time experience. Because oxytocin is only released in response to a stimulus, it can't be faked. This not only predicts how a person might act, but it also helps marketers identify the pieces of the ad that are most engaging or falling flat. It is a scientific view of the art of storytelling, showing what our brains value most.

I put my TED Talk through an experiment on the Immersion software. I figured I would see the most engagement and oxytocin spikes during the opening and closing stories. What resulted was very different. One spot demonstrated a consistent spike in engagement across viewers: when I described Antonio Damasio's research with patients who had brain damage and were unable to make decisions. I described neuroscience in story form. The combination of the story, unexpected elements, and the stakes of decision-making created an engagement spike. It was new, unexpected information that slowed down the assumptions of my audience.

It isn't enough to tell a story. The way we construct the story to maximize the brain's attention and engagement directly impacts the experience of the story and the likelihood of achieving the desired outcome. To achieve what you want your audience to know, think, do, or feel, you must tell a story that connects to emotions. Through neuroscience research, we know there is a difference between telling a story and telling a *great* story.

WHAT MAKES A GREAT STORY?

Great stories have three key elements: characters, conflict, and connection. They also culminate in an outcome for the audience—something they know, feel, think, or do differently because of the story. Within each great story, concepts from the Five Factory Settings of the Brain are applied to intentionally increase immersion and engagement.

Characters

Your characters need two things: to be relatable and to have conflict. The audience wants to have a sense of who the characters are and why they do what they do, even if they don't like them or agree with them. We can learn a lot from the mistakes and failures people make. You don't have to have a hero. But you do want characters your audience can recognize.

Great storytellers describe "the truth" of a story, or what is real about the story. They answer questions like, *How will the audience connect to the story? Are there events and actions that feel real and true to what they know?* Characters illustrate these truths through their actions.

Characters also move a story forward, often through the conflict they have with others and themselves. This creates tension and something to resolve. Describe the arc the character experiences as they learn, grow, and change through the story. Include the character's decisions and demonstrate what they value. Use specific details, metaphors, and examples to make their actions relatable. As you craft your own story, decide if your characters help your audience feel part of an "in-group" or "out-group."

Conflict

The heart of every story includes something that happens and changes everything. It's the point of the story. This is the fuel source that the story is structured around. When you run out of conflict, you run out of story.

Conflict is inherent with tension. You want to build toward conflict in a way that is unexpected, slows assumptions, and makes the brain spend calories. This is done through surprising plot points, details, outcomes, or even unexpected metaphors within the story.

Characters often have conflict with themselves or each other. Describe what is at stake and needs to be resolved. Show the arc of who characters are before and after the conflict. Consider if the actions of your characters make your audience feel enjoyable or uncomfortable—like dropping their phone down an elevator shaft.

Connection

A great story intentionally engages the audience's senses. We should see, hear, feel, smell, taste, and experience the same things as the characters. Include specific details to help anchor what the audience knows and aid in their recall. Create empathy and curiosity with descriptions of characters, their challenges, and their choices. Connect the audience to emotion to help with decision-making and the desired outcome. We want them to feel sadness, happiness, fear, frustration, anger, surprise, and disgust.

Culmination

Each story has a most wanted outcome. It may be a new idea, feeling, or increased awareness. You want your audience to do or decide something. Commercials make us want to buy products or services. Movie trailers make us choose to see the movie. Charities seek increased awareness, activism, and donations. A great story is built to achieve the desired outcome from the audience through the characters, connections, and conflicts.

The science of storytelling helps you understand what will engage the brain as you create your stories. Thoughtfully leveraging the Five Factory Settings in each story helps connect the audience to the desired outcome and hack the art of storytelling. The past chapters help you understand the why of the storytelling methodology. Now it's time to learn how to do each thing described.

Great stories aren't born fully baked. They begin with a fragment of an idea and are developed through ongoing creation and refinement. Creating a toolkit of ideas gives you an inventory well before you ever have a need to tell a story. The next chapter shows you how.

SUMMARY

Creating Desired Outcomes

See the checklists in the back of the book.

- The way a story is told makes a difference in the experience and engagement.
- Stories build empathy and trust. As we listen to stories, we develop empathy, leading to a measurable spike in oxytocin. The more oxytocin that is released, the more trustworthy we perceive the storyteller.
- Data doesn't change our behavior; our emotions do.
- Sensory experiences are stamped with emotions. Those experiences are called upon to inform future predictions for similar situations.
- Most decision-making happens unconsciously. At the point we become aware of a decision, we apply logic, making us think we are choosing rational decisions.
- Stories that don't build and release tension, create an arc, or are too predictable often don't create high engagement for the audience.
- Great stories include:
  - Relatable characters. We understand why they do what they do, even if we don't agree or like them.
  - Building and releasing of conflict, tension, and increasing stakes.
  - Culmination in the most wanted outcome.
  - Immersion of the audience by engaging senses and emotions.
  - Understanding created by anchoring to what is already known, often with metaphors.
  - Unexpected plot points, details, and outcomes.
  - Identification as a member of an in-group or out-group by the audience.

Dr. Paul Zak

Neuroscientist, Founder of Immersion Neuroscience,
and Professor at Claremont Graduate University

Where do you start your storytelling process?

I start with the headline. Why would anyone care about this and give me time? Your audience is either going to listen or read what you've created or watch cat videos. How can I add value, keep their attention, and make it worth their while?

Writing allows me to understand the core idea of the piece. Get it out, chop it up, polish it, and make it beautiful. That process causes a little gem to appear. I need to seduce you into continuing to read. I do that by using weird punctuation, signs and symbols, and keywords that produce a particular image in the audience's brain.

For example, I had a *Psychology Today* blog. I wrote one post called "How to Run a Con," about getting conned out of money from the cash drawer of the gas station where I worked. It wasn't an "I'm awesome" post. It was a self-effacing piece: "I was a dumb kid, let's go through the neuroscience of this experience." That vulnerable piece got 250,000 views.

When do you test your stories?

Because I have access to the Immersion software, I will send out a five-minute recording around the third draft. A panel listens, and the Immersion software measures brain responses. I can line up the measurement to precise moments in the recording. Most people are nice, and they don't give useful feedback if you ask them. This cuts through that.

What do you consider when editing?

An editor once told me, "You need to express what the reader needs to know, not what you need to write." Sometimes stories fall flat when the writer loves them, but the reader doesn't get it.

I'm a big believer in editors. I've rebooted my brain to embrace revisions as a chance to create beauty in the world. Get it out there, throw out a lot, or maybe start over. Put it away, sleep on it, and come back to it.

I want to create as much value as possible for the reader. Can I compress this into six hundred or eight hundred words and really make it rock? Is everything explained well? Is it jargon-free? There is constant polishing. For many articles, I've done seventy drafts.

I look for an internal feeling, like a muse speaking through me. You can surprise yourself with, "I don't know how this came out of my brain, but it's good!" That sounds weird, but it's the best!

What habits have you implemented?

I schedule time on my calendar for writing. I am also a big believer in walks without music or a book. That movement makes you open to what is happening. Try out ideas on people you trust. Get feedback so you don't repeat mistakes.

There is a lot of internal resistance and critiques we have of ourselves, that we are not good writers. The more you do it, the better you get. So, turn off the internal critique machine and have fun!

PART TWO

The Context

Finding Ideas for Stories

FOUR

Create an Endless Toolkit
of Potential Story Ideas

Vanessa is the CEO of a small, multinational tech company. While dispersed across the globe, the company had an office-centric culture. Everyone was used to working in the office to collaborate and connect. That is, until COVID-19 forced the company to quickly pivot to virtual work.

During the first few weeks, Vanessa sent out messages about logistics and how employees could get help if needed. By the third week, she realized she needed to meaningfully connect with employees beyond logistics. They were concerned about their families and loved ones staying healthy. Many were also helping their kids participate in school at home. The world-in-limbo left employees concerned about their jobs and the company's survival.

Vanessa knew storytelling was a great way to connect with employees. The problem was, she was taught there are four types of stories you need to be able to tell. Employees didn't need to hear the company's origin story or a story about their success. They needed to hear stories about trust, resilience, hope, and overcoming challenges. Stories she had never thought about or developed. She realized she needed a bunch of story ideas that she could use in weekly messages to employees.

When Vanessa first reached out to me for help, we talked through different employee challenges. I asked her questions that prompted her to think of specific examples. At first, the ideas were slow to come. Then, the more she came up with, the faster and easier they flowed. As she talked, I typed. Within minutes, she had brainstormed twenty-five different ideas. Some were personal stories. Some were experiences from client interactions. And others were from articles and podcasts she had recently consumed.

Vanessa knew she did her best thinking on walks. We set up her list of story ideas in an app she could access on her phone. Anytime she thought of a new idea, she could easily add it to keep them in one place. This became her toolkit. She scanned these ideas to find one that supported the theme she wanted to focus on in that week's message.

For six months, Vanessa sent a weekly email to employees with stories. Views increased by 60 percent and interactions by 78 percent. Employees discussed the stories on their teams and replied directly to her with their own stories. This office-centric culture realized they could maintain connections through stories, even when virtual. The company sustained its double-digit growth and looked forward to the weekly stories.

Each Friday, Vanessa spent ten minutes capturing ideas for stories, expanding her toolkit to over fifty ideas. She no longer struggled to find ideas. Many weeks she didn't even need to her use her toolkit. Interactions with employees helped her see the theme and outcome she wanted to focus on, and the ideas for stories would emerge in real time.

COLLECTING STORY IDEAS

Do you ever wonder, *Where am I going to find ideas for stories?* Or, *I'm afraid I will quickly run out of story ideas.* This can feel paralyzing. The heavier this thought sits, the harder it becomes to find ideas and the faster you abandon telling a story. The challenge isn't finding the story idea. It's adopting the right mindset and habits to create an endless list of ideas. Collecting ideas is an ongoing process—something you want to do regularly before ever needing to tell a story. Start by identifying your mindset for discovering ideas.

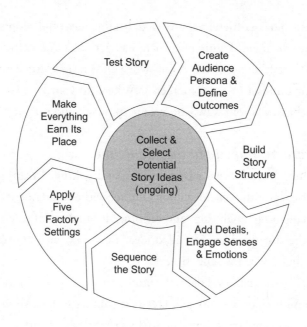

How do you find your best story ideas?

I love asking storytellers, "How do you find your best story ideas?" Each has experimented to find what works best for them. Taking walks, reading articles, listening to podcasts, having conversations, looking at pictures, searching the internet, and reflecting on personal or professional experiences are just a few places they explore.

Chris Brogan is a strategic advisor and speaker. He takes a mental note of things that intrigue him as he moves through the day—like a funny moment from a meeting or interaction. He collects things that catch his attention so he can weave them into a story at any given moment.

Caitlin Weaver is an author who notices specific moments in her life: a sweet interaction with her kids or a problem weighing on her. She leans into these moments, using her writing to make sense of why that moment is sticking in her head.

You may not think of stories as data-driven, but advertising executive Colby Webb does. She analyzes consumer, company, and cultural data specific to audiences, products, and behaviors. The data-informed insights are leveraged to create personalized, meaningful marketing and stories for individual consumers at scale.

Each person has a different approach to finding ideas and adopts a mindset when looking for them. Figure out where you get ideas and define your own approach. What have you been doing when inspiration struck in the past? What is your mindset in these moments? Where do your best ideas come to you? The right way is *your* way. Know your approach and call on it.

You can't create and edit at the same time.

Storytelling includes two parts: creating and editing. Creating is expansive. It involves building one idea upon another without judgment or critique. Editing is tightening, analyzing, and refining. It questions if something contributes to the story and the intended idea. Both play an important role in storytelling, but not at the same time.

Neuroscience research validates the more you are relaxed and let your mind wander, the more brain activity and creativity you have (Raichle and Mintun 2006). As pressure and stress increase, so does the release of cortisol and adrenaline to intentionally narrow your focus. Your ability to generate creative ideas becomes much harder.

The best time to come up with a potential idea for a story is when you don't need it. Regularly collect ideas—or even fragments of ideas—for things that catch your interest. Capture ideas without editing yourself by questioning, *How will I tell this story for my audience?* You want to generate ideas without a home in mind. Great storytellers don't wait until it's time to tell a story to come up with one. They collect things that inspire them along the way and review them when it's time to tell a story.

Gather a list of ideas on an ongoing basis. Don't worry about how or when you will use them. Simply pay attention to those things that fascinate you. You will soon recognize the endless story ideas for your toolkit.

You don't need a fully baked story. You just need an idea.

Improv actors don't have a full scene scripted. They build on ideas with the support of others. The fifteen-minute set a comedian does comes from a small moment from everyday life—not a fully formed narrative. The same principle applies to storytelling. You aren't looking for fully formed stories. You're focusing on finding ideas, pieces, moments, details, fragments, metaphors . . . even photos you can later piece together to form a story for a specific need.

As you move through the world, notice the things that catch your attention. I often experience a nagging feeling when I encounter an idea. I don't know how or when I will use it, but I know that feeling is an indication to capture the idea. Notice what captures your attention and add it to your list. The energy, excitement, or fascination you have for an idea will come through in the story.

Where will you capture ideas?

Figure out a place to capture your story ideas. Inspiration will hit at the oddest moment, and you want to have a place to store the idea. Don't try to hold it in your head. I learned this the hard way. My best ideas come during walks or hikes. I would boastfully convince myself I would remember the idea at the end of the walk. Once I got back to my laptop, my mind was blank.

I started out capturing ideas with a small notebook and a pen. Over time, I moved to an online document and then an app. This lets me access the list from any device or location. I periodically move them into a spreadsheet for a master list that I can categorize, sort, and note when they've been used. Identifying a place to capture ideas helps you generate more of them.

You may want a notebook, an app, or a spreadsheet file. You may be a visual thinker and want to collect photos that trigger thinking. Perhaps scraps of paper and Post-its work best. Maybe you have an inventory you update regularly. Designate one central place where you can capture ideas. This will be the same place you will later return when choosing an idea for a story. The goal is to have a system to free your mind to think of more ideas, not spend energy trying to remember them—or remember where you put them.

Don't worry about collecting full-blown stories. Collect pieces of ideas or things you find fascinating. I recently read an article about the origin of air bag design being informed by origami. I also saw a disco ball in a retirement home. Both of those ideas got added to my list. I don't know how or when I will use them, but I find something intriguing about each.

You may want to include a few notes about why the idea excited you to help you later remember what it means. Some people add a theme categorization, so they can filter by topic when searching for story ideas. Do whatever works best for you.

Stories come through constraint.

Great storytellers don't have perfected stories in their back pockets. They know that ideas don't magically appear. Instead, they have created a habit to curate ideas for their toolkit on an ongoing basis, well before they need a story.

| Constraints aren't limiting; they provide focus. |

Creativity comes from two things: mindset and focus. Creativity isn't about casting a broad net. It's about digging deep into a specific topic. Your best ideas will be discovered when you apply constraints within a specific context. Constraints aren't limiting; they provide focus.

The most dreaded question in a job interview is, "Tell me about yourself." It's so broad and vague—where do you start? If the question was "Tell me what you liked about your last job" or "Describe a project you were proud of," you would have plenty to share. The same thing happens in storytelling. If we don't apply constraints, our brains don't know which file to access to retrieve an idea. Our mind goes blank for what feels like an awkwardly long time. Ask a specific question, and the brain immediately becomes focused and can access memories and ideas.

If I ask you, "Tell me about your childhood," you may tell me the city you grew up in, the type of housing you had, and the number of siblings and relatives you grew up with. Your response would be general because your childhood is full of endless stories and experiences. That question is too broad to tap into them.

Change the question to "What sound or smell reminds you of home?" and you can recall many stories. You may describe the chime of the grandfather clock that had been in your family for three generations and was always seven minutes late. Or you would describe the two-layer sourdough chocolate cake with walnuts and chocolate icing that was made with love for every family birthday.

If you asked me, "When was a time you laughed uncontrollably?" I'd tell you how the smell of red wine reminds me of the time the cork broke when my mom tried to open a bottle. We wrestled with the bottle for two minutes before the remaining cork plunged inside. Wine exploded out and sprayed everywhere. Purple splatters covered the ceiling like a Jackson Pollock painting. We both ended up drenched and belly laughing.

Ideas come from digging into specific questions and details. The more constraints you apply, the easier and longer the list of story ideas you can generate.

CREATING YOUR TOOLKIT

The television writer's room is the birthplace of the stories and character arcs of your favorite shows. The walls are covered with notecards and random phrases. Each represents an idea: an experience, emotion, or event for a character or storyline. The ideas exist as orphans, waiting to be incorporated into a character or story.

As the writers talk through the development of different episodes, they review these ideas, weighing if any should be included in the storyline. Some cards get included immediately; others are stuck on the island of misfit ideas for the entirety of the series, never receiving a home. These are a key part of the writer's toolkit. They serve as story ideas to give a starting point during the season.

Create your story idea toolkit. This will be the first thing you reference for ideas and inspiration each time you are telling a story. Build this before you ever need a story. It will be easier to brainstorm ideas when you aren't facing a deadline for a specific story. Use the various prompts to trigger thinking. You may choose to answer questions that intrigue you or use them to trigger your ideas. The prompts help narrow your focus to stimulate an abundance and depth of ideas.

The first time you create the toolkit, it works best when you sit in a different chair or location to tap into your creative thinking. Plan at least twenty minutes for this first list building. Your ideas may be slow to form, but the more you capture, the faster they will flow. Don't worry about how or if you will use an idea. Gather words, sentences, or phrases with enough information that will make sense when you later review them.

The questions that follow are prompts to spark thinking. Not every question will resonate with you. Focus on those that feel meaningful and inspire ideas. Capture additional ideas that also arise.

Your Personal Experiences

Your personal life has many rich moments and lessons that could contribute to a story. Personal experiences don't mean private moments or oversharing, but they do mean including your perspective. Capture specific moments, ideas, and realizations from your experiences.

- What is a defining event in your life?
- What was a situation that didn't start funny, but you now laugh about?
- What would do differently if you were able?
- What did you learn from a vacation adventure?
- What pets did you have growing up?
- What is a hidden talent of yours?
- Who was your favorite teacher?
- What was your first concert, car, or date?
- Have you had a car break down? What did you learn?
- What would you save if your home was on fire?
- What is the best advice you've received?
- What is a skill or talent you mastered?
- What traditions were observed in your home?
- What is something you should have thrown out but can't part with?
- Ask a friend or family member:
  - What is your favorite thing about me?
  - What was I like as a child?
  - What did you imagine I would do for a living?

Your Professional Experiences

What are the key moments from your professional life? Your career has rich insights for stories: first-time experiences, lessons learned, and achievements. I could focus on my professional career and never run out of stories sharing realizations and learnings. Use the list below as a starting point to capture story ideas from your career. As you work through the questions, capture other ideas that emerge. Specific moments from projects, coaching conversations, or mistakes are often rich story ideas.

- What was your first job?
- What was a mistake or failure you learned from?
- What was a difficult team or project you experienced?
- What change made you afraid of losing or gaining something?
- Who was your best or worst leader?
- What is a moment where you thought, *This is why I do this work!*
- When was a moment when you had no idea what you were doing?
- What is something you would like to do over?
- What would you tell the younger version of yourself?
- What are you most proud of?
- What is the best advice you have received?

Look at Customers, Clients, and Stakeholders

Henry owns a brand and web design company. He recognized that most entrepreneurs struggle to describe their products and services in a compelling way. He developed a process to help entrepreneurs define their brand and ideal clients before building them a new website.

Henry reached out to me for help as he planned stories for the launch of his signature process. I asked him questions about the problems his clients mentioned. He described their frustrations of no longer wanting to be a best-kept secret. Many had a strong desire to attract qualified leads and build steady revenue. Henry's clients weren't seeking websites; they wanted help in realizing their business goals.

We developed a series of stories that described different clients who faced similar challenges. These involved Henry taking them through his signature process to help each level-up their business. Future clients saw their own problems in the stories, telling Henry they felt like they were written about them.

Look at customers, clients, and stakeholders for story ideas. Interactions, challenges, testimonials, and questions each represent potential stories. If your client or stakeholder experiences it, others will as well. They'll see themselves in stories about frustrations, hopes, dreams, and fears and feel as though you're speaking directly to them.

- What problems do your customers face? What do they complain about?
- What do your clients aspire to be, do, or have in the future?
- What pain points you have solved for your clients?
- What do customers say they love about your product or solution? Why?
- How do your clients find you?
- What challenges would you find of your customers if you searched online?
- What have you learned from the evolution of your product or solutions?
- What are the seven principles or ideas your clients need to know?
- Why did you start your products and/or services?

Find a Muse

Sally is one of my muses. As the head of HR of a Fortune 500 company, she embodies many of my clients. I call her when I feel stuck and want to get ideas. I listen to her challenges and frustrations as a leader. As she describes the problems she grapples with, the story ideas pile up. I know if Sally faces these things as a leader, others do too. I generally keep five different muses that represent my audience at any given time. A muse can be someone who connects you to the challenges of your audience. Or it can be someone who sparks your creative process.

- What would make someone your ideal customer?
- What problems do they struggle with?
- How have you helped them, and what did they realize in the process?
- Where have they had success?

- What comes easily to them?
- Where are they looking to grow?
- What aspirations do they have?

In the World

Great ideas may come to us as we move through the world. Anything that captures your interest, excitement, or reflection should be noted, even if you aren't clear why. The day Maria dropped her phone down the elevator, I knew it was an interesting idea. It wasn't until I read the article about Walt Bettinger that I recognized how it could become a story. As you move through the world, take note of those things that catch your attention.

- What is a favorite movie or piece of art that moves you? Why?
- What music can you play endlessly?
- What topics can you talk about all day?
- What is an outdoor space you love to visit?
- Have you ever heard the origin of a product or a company that stuck with you?
- Do you have a favorite museum?
- Is there an article or podcast episode that stood out to you? Why?
- What is your favorite city or place to visit? Why?
- Do you have a favorite book?
- Have you heard a speech or speaker that stayed with you?

Passage of Time

In 1936, Carl Mayer got an idea to design a 13-foot hot dog on wheels to transport the company spokesman. This "Wienermobile" was driven around Chicago advertising Oscar Mayer hot dogs. Over the years that followed, the Wienermobile expanded to a fleet of six vehicles. Each is driven by two "Hot Doggers," recent university graduates who compete to win the coveted spots traveling the US for a year.

The Wienermobile is an anchor of time travel and nostalgia, full of endless stories that could be told. The first time someone saw the Wienermobile. A day-in-the-life of the Hot Doggers. Memories of a guest seeing the Wienermobile with a loved one who has passed away. Chauffeuring a bride and groom from their wedding to their reception. Small towns printing photos of the Wienermobile next to landmarks in their local papers. Or even changes in the world over the eighty-plus years since the first Wienermobile was created. By using the Wienermobile as the anchor, it allows you to dig into endless details and ideas.

Look for story ideas in the people, places, or objects that bear witness to the passage of time by how people interact with them. In the past forty years, the evolution of the phone has included rotary dials, push buttons hanging on the wall with long cords, cordless, flip phones, and smartphones. There are so many different stories that could be told over the passage of that time, both about the phone itself and about all the different things that have happened over those years—from world events to changes in individual lives.

Add to your toolkit of story ideas by building a list of things that serve as an anchor and reference to the passage of time.

- Is there a conference room or building in your workplace that has witnessed different meetings or events over the years?
- Did you have a stuffed animal, blanket, lucky charm, or piece of clothing that followed you on multiple experiences?
- Is there any object that has been passed down through your family?
- What are objects in your day-to-day that have evolved over the passage and time (e.g., rotary phone to mobile phone)?
- What are different world events your audience witnessed over their lifetime?
- What is an object that could tell multiple points of experience? For example, my hiking boots are twenty-five years old. They represent many stories of the different hikes, trips to different countries, and life events.

How to Keep This List Fresh

The more ideas you have in your toolkit, the easier it is to choose one to turn into your perfect story. Start with the prompts to build a list for your toolkit. Then regularly dedicate time to add to it. Capture any article or a conversation that leaves you inspired. Challenge yourself to add an idea each day or set a weekly reminder to update your toolkit. Once you start adding ideas, the more you will notice them and recognize when your curiosity is piqued. Getting started is the hardest part. Once you start capturing ideas, there is a compounding effect.

What If You Get Writer's Block?

Struggling to come up with ideas feels like flipping through your closet of clothes and not finding anything to wear. What do you do in these moments?

Remember: the relaxed brain is the most creative. Try not to back yourself against a deadline of having to tell a story without any ideas to share. Leave space for creativity. Recognize the story won't just come to you. You will need to go do some work to tap into ideas. Where have your previous ideas for stories come from? What were you doing? Who can you talk with that will help spark ideas?

Which questions do you get most often? We are so close to our areas of expertise that we often overlook things that might create meaningful stories for people looking to learn more. Think through the common questions and conversations you encounter, and see what ideas pop up. Try experimenting with AI searches on the questions you frequently receive. Capture your reaction to the results as potential ideas.

Photos can be a great source of inspiration. If I am trying to figure out a story on trust, I may search online for "trust" and look at images. Stock photo websites can be great sources to trigger thinking. I also will scroll through my camera roll, which also helps prompt memories from my own experiences.

I was recently giving a keynote to Microsoft. I needed to figure out an opening story but didn't have any obvious ideas. I've learned in these moments to trust the process. The group wanted to learn how to use stories to better engage with their customers. I asked myself, *What is an idea that reinforces the theme of connection?* Then I went for a walk. By the end of that walk, not only had I come up with an idea for the opening story, I added two more ideas into my toolkit. Walking always unlocks ideas for me that don't reveal themselves when I am behind my laptop.

Building your toolkit of ideas isn't the same thing as picking an idea for a story. It's about tapping into your creative process to generate a rich inventory of ideas. The toolkit of ideas brings you to the starting line of the storytelling process. An idea has no home without an audience. Each story begins with understanding your audience and what you want them to take away from the story—even before you know the story you want to tell. That is where we'll go next: how to get clear on your audience so your story can speak directly to them.

─ SUMMARY ─

Create an Endless Toolkit of Potential Story Ideas

See the checklists in the back of the book.

- Explore how you find your best story ideas.
- In storytelling, you can't create and edit at the same time.
- Identify ideas for stories before you ever need to tell a story. Create a habit of doing this when you're relaxed and build a toolkit of ideas.
- Capture ideas, not fully baked stories. They're fragments, metaphors, or even pictures.
- Define a place to capture story ideas, like an app or a notebook. Don't rely on your brain to remember it later.
- Story ideas emerge when you apply constraints. Prompts, questions, categories, and moments can help you identify ideas for stories.
- Create a toolkit of ideas. See the checklist at the end of the book for consolidated prompts:
  - Personal experiences
  - Professional experiences
  - Challenges, aspirations, and experiences of customers, clients, and stakeholders
  - Insights from a muse
  - Things that catch your attention in the world
  - Items or locations that can anchor to time and changes over the years
- Building your toolkit of ideas isn't the same thing as picking an idea for a story. Focus on building a list of ideas without knowing when or where it will be told.

Gary Ware

Improv Comedian, Author, and Workshop Facilitator

How does improv relate to storytelling?

Improv is storytelling in collaboration with others. In improv, "we" is greater than "me." You must be able to surrender and know the result is going to be something you never would have thought of on your own. That can be scary. It isn't perfect, and it can be messy. And I love going through the process.

How do you get ideas for stories or improv?

There are two states we create from: the clown and the editor. The clown allows you to experiment and generate ideas without a filter. The editor comes in later to find the gems and do cleanup. But you can't be the clown and the editor at the same time. There will be time to refine and revise. If you don't get things out, you won't have anything to revise.

"Yes, and . . ." is a fundamental principle of improv. Each person builds on ideas contributed, regardless of what they are or who they came from. If someone says, "Let's take a vacation to the beach!", you might respond, "Perfect, I have a new orange beach towel!" This builds on the initial idea and creates openness and space for others. If you responded, "I don't like the beach," you shut down thinking and ideas. "Yes, and . . ." invites possibility. It may feel messy, but this is the best part of creation. Lean into that discomfort.

Where do people get stuck?

When I teach improv, I notice people often feel like they must bring every possible idea into a scene. That can feel very overwhelming, especially when you don't know where to start. I begin by asking, "What is one idea you can bring?" As they offer one, I then ask, "What is another little thing you can contribute?"

This is how stories are built, compiling ideas along a story structure. A storytelling model provides parameters that free up creativity. I use prompts to help generate ideas: "Tell me about a time you went on vacation." I'll build on that by asking, "Describe this vacation to your inner five-year-old child." It becomes a different story. While the plot points may stay the same, the details, descriptions, and delivery differ. We hold ourselves back out of fear of being judged. People need help letting go of that mindset.

What advice would you give about storytelling?

In improv, everything is a gift. You're always looking for offers to build on. If a scene partner says "Wow, I am so tired," then my job is to build on that. My response must answer the question "If this is true, what else is true?" The audience is also part of the ensemble and story. My best days as an improviser are when someone says, "What do you mean that wasn't scripted?" It's all about trusting, responding, and having fun.

FIVE

Start with Your Audience, Not with the Story

My phone flashed with cascading text messages from my client Riley, the head of HR for a Fortune 500 healthcare business.

"I have a presentation next week, and I want to start with a story. I am thinking of the one about my friend from college who failed an exam that put her at risk of not graduating. Or should I tell the story about that manager who said something offensive, and no one reacted? What about the story of the woman who made her point using sock puppets? Which story is your favorite?"

These were Riley's greatest hits—the stories she loved to tell. "It doesn't matter which one is your favorite or my favorite," I replied. "What matters is what your audience needs to hear."

She replied with the eye-rolling emoji. "Just tell me what story I should tell."

"What do you want your audience to know, think, feel, or do after the presentation? Until you figure that out, you can't select a story. Your favorite story may not resonate with your audience. It's like music. If I gave you a playlist with my favorite songs, you wouldn't love each one. Specific ones resonate."

Stories that fall flat or seem pointless often share one thing in common. They center on the storyteller and what they love about the story—neglecting to make it meaningful for the audience. It's as if you don't have to be there.

They're so wrapped up in their story, they forget the point is to connect the listener to an idea or a feeling.

The secret of storytelling is that it doesn't start with the story; it starts with the audience. This allows the storyteller to put the audience in the center of the story and intentionally weave in things that are meaningful to them. This makes the audience feel the storyteller is speaking directly to them. A great story begins with understanding the audience and the desired outcome.

> The secret of storytelling is that it doesn't start with the story; it starts with the audience.

The way you tell a story will vary based on each audience. If I were telling the story about dropping a phone down an elevator shaft to a group of security guards, I would tell it differently. I might take Ray's perspective, describing how disheartening it is to have people walk past each morning without barely a nod. I'd share looking forward to seeing Maria each day—the one person who stops to say hello. I'd describe how talking to Maria makes my day because she knows my name and remembers my last vacation. When Maria drops her phone, I'd describe this nagging feeling—wanting to figure out how to help her get it back. The basic plot may be the same, but the details, the order, the perspective, and the takeaways would differ. Just like an image changes when twisting a kaleidoscope, one story could be told many ways to focus on different perspectives and connections. Defining the audience helps identify different perspectives and details to incorporate into the story so it feels as if it were personally written for them.

You often hear the advice, "Write to one person." This is another way of saying, "Start with your audience!" Be specific, as if the person were sitting across the table from you drinking a cup of coffee. Use examples and details that person will understand. Any quips, metaphors, or examples you would use in a coffee conversation should be the same that you bring into the story. Each directly impacts how well the story creates a connection and resonates. This also works in an audience of different people by defining personas.

DEFINE A PERSONA

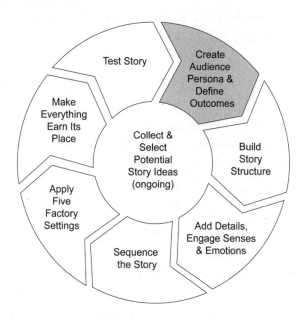

Personas are fictional characters that embody the traits, experiences, and thoughts of your audience. Marketing uses personas to target messaging for products and services. Movies and TV shows use personas when writing their content to make sure the stories resonate with their audience. Personas are even used in the creation of business processes, apps, and websites to help plan the user's experience. These help you picture the audience sitting across the table from you so you can speak directly to the details, experiences, and motivation that are most meaningful to them.

Each time you tell a story, your audience has at least one persona. Even though the audience may be made of different ages, backgrounds, and experiences, they share something in common that brings them together. Start by defining a persona for the entire audience. Name your persona. Include specific details. If your persona has a habit of getting a latte on Thursdays, note that. It can be used when building out the story to connect to what people already know and understand.

Build a persona by answering the questions that feel relevant to your audience. This is meant to be a quick exercise—something that you can do in about five minutes. Long enough to think of specific details and get an image of your audience, and short enough that you aren't hung up on the details and lose momentum building your story.

- What brings this group of people together to be your audience?
- What do they have in common?
- What is the average age of your audience?
- What is the education experience of your audience?
- What type of role or expertise do they hold?
- Where does your audience live?
- What hobbies does your audience participate in?
- What does a typical day look like for them?

What happens if you have multiple personas in your audience?

As I prepared to give my TED Talk, I realized I had two different personas for my audience. One was the university students in the theater where I would give the talk. The other was leaders and employees in corporations who would see the recorded talk. I needed to engage the students in the theater to create energy in the room—otherwise the video would fall flat. I kept flip-flopping my focus from the audience in the room to those who would watch the video—until I built out their personas.

Grace is my student persona. She is a twenty-one-year-old undergraduate who holds a part-time job. She is pursuing a data analytics certificate in addition to her major to help with job prospects upon graduation. Grace doesn't have a lot of storytelling experience and often sits in boring, data-heavy, unmemorable lectures. When not in class, Grace loves online gaming. She is active in animal rescue and human rights causes. In between classes, she orders a coffee from an app on her phone that is delivered by a robot. Grace's first class is at 8:00 a.m. She meets friends for lunch at noon and finishes her classes by 3 p.m. She studies until 7 p.m. when she grabs a poke bowl for dinner on the way to a fundraising meeting for the local animal shelter. After the meeting, she gets a text from friends to join them at Harry's, the local bar.

Darren is the persona of my corporate leader. He is between thirty to fifty-five years old. His work experience ranges from seven to twenty-five years. He's worked at two companies and has at least one employee he manages. He has a bachelor's degree and is married with two children. His nephew has autism, and his extended family gets together most weekends. He has minimal experience with storytelling, relying on data for his presentations. Darren's day begins with a cycling class before work at 6 a.m. After, he feeds his kids breakfast and gets them ready for school. He is at work by 8:45 a.m. and spends forty-five minutes responding to emails before starting back-to-back meetings. He then spends two hours creating PowerPoint slides full of charts for an upcoming presentation. Instead of planning what he wants to say, he flips through existing content to see what he can leverage. Throughout the day he periodically picks up his phone, checking texts from his wife, friends, and colleagues. On his drive home, he calls his brother and checks in on his nephew. He has spaghetti with his family and watches a TV show before going to bed.

I could have split Darren's persona into additional ones for entrepreneurs and people who focus on data analytics, but that nuance wasn't necessary. The big difference between the two was that one was a full-time student and the other was a full-time employee. Mobile phones play a huge role in both of their lives, and both are regularly in situations that have a bias for data and an opportunity to increase storytelling.

Outlining a day-in-the-life captures specific details of your persona. Some may even find their way into the story later. The combination of the questions and day-in-the-life snapshot helps reinforce what is clear and unknown about the audience. Even if you don't use all the details, both help you gain clarity on your audience and inform the desired outcome.

GET IN THE AUDIENCE'S MIND

A story has a desired outcome—whether entertaining your audience, shifting their thinking, teaching them something new, or inspiring action. Each time you tell a story (or communicate information), ask yourself these four questions to define your audience and the desired outcome. Don't skip this step, even if you already know the story you want to tell.

1. What do you want the audience to know or think because of the story?
2. What do you want them to feel or do because of the story?
3. What is their current mindset?
4. What might be an obstacle in getting the audience to think, feel, or act differently?

The questions help specify what you want your audience to experience in a story or communication. These meet the audience where they are and address potential obstacles. They bring clarity and focus to the story and outcome you are creating. The questions are intentionally simplistic and meant to be answered within a few minutes. Use them whether you're telling a story in the next ten minutes or next week.

I am often asked if I have experience telling stories for a specific industry like sales, finance, or tech. People hear me tell stories for one audience and want to make sure I have relevant stories for their audience. This is the beauty of the process. It works for any context.

These four questions have helped me recognize the need to ground an audience in the neuroscience of trust for a leadership keynote at an engineering conference. They have also helped me illustrate what happens when you neglect to engage senses in a storytelling keynote for a creative company. They help you get specific on what each audience needs. Even when you're telling the same story to different audiences, the questions help you identify how to tailor the story to meet each desired outcome.

Sometimes you may tell a story to connect people to the idea of something that won't be realized for some time. The pharmaceutical and medical industries treat illnesses that may take many months to show results. The story can become the glue between starting treatment and seeing results over time. Sales connect people to things they want to be, do, or have through products and services. Stories connect the buyer to the "I want that!" aspiration. They can also help bring context to data to support a discussion or decision. The role and purpose of the story will vary for each audience. Ensure your story is meaningful by defining the audience, desired outcomes, and potential obstacles.

Back in the Elevator...

I defined desired outcomes for each of my personas for the TED Talk. I wanted to see the overlap for the story.

1. **What do you want the audience to know or think differently?**

   I wanted Grace to recognize that most of her class lectures weren't dynamic or memorable. Stories could help her become a memorable communicator in any context.

   My goal for Darren was to challenge the belief he should only communicate data in presentations. I wanted him to recognize how stories can bring meaning to data and that he didn't have to trade one for the other.

   I wanted both Grace and Darren to recognize the science behind storytelling. That it isn't a soft skill, but a smarter way of communicating to engage the brain. While their application may differ, the goal for both was recognizing that stories create more trust, understanding, and meaning for the listener.

2. **What do you want them to feel or do differently?**

   I wanted Grace to come away inspired to try storytelling in class presentations to become a dynamic and memorable communicator in her career.

   My goal for Darren was for him to experiment using storytelling with data and in his presentations to be more influential and memorable.

   I wanted both Grace and Darren to feel inspired to leverage storytelling and experience the feeling of helping an audience see something you can no longer "unsee" to shift understanding and perception.

3. **What is their current mindset?**

   Grace doesn't realize storytelling is compelling in business presentations and sharing data. She hasn't seen it role-modeled by professors.

Each of her data analytics classes talks about how data is facts and necessary to make informed decisions. Grace tells stories on social media, but it hasn't occurred to her to use them in presentations.

Darren's company is undergoing a data transformation. Employees are encouraged to make data-driven decisions, but no one knows what that means. There are many quality issues with the data. Darren believes that data is more factual than stories. The few times he was encouraged to "Tell a story!", he avoided it. He couldn't think of one to tell and decided it wasn't worth the risk of being perceived as manipulative.

Both Darren and Grace think that data is fact and stories aren't. To shift their mindsets, I needed to address this belief.

4. **What might be an obstacle for your audience?**

The obstacles are similar for the different personas. Both have the mindset that data is fact and stories are fluff. They may hesitate to communicate differently than their peers and be hesitant to use storytelling for more effective outcomes.

They also share the challenge of not knowing where to find stories or how to tell them. Their perceptions of storytelling may be stuck in the belief that if you're telling a story, you're sharing personal details—and they aren't comfortable with that.

Creating the two personas and working through the questions helped me find the overlap in both. Their day-to-day lives are different, but their mindset on storytelling isn't. Neither is fully aware of the science behind storytelling or how stories bring meaning to data. Before creating the personas, I was guilty of putting myself in the center. I kept thinking of stories I loved to tell and how I could make them fit. I wasn't considering what the audience needed to hear. Once I defined the personas and answered the four questions, I saw my mistake and the stories became clear.

Start with your audience. Create the persona(s). Define what you want them to know, think, feel, or do differently. Specify the outcome and what obstacles may lay in the path. It will put your audience at the center and create a foundation for your story.

You select the idea for your story only after you are clear on your audience and the outcome you want them to have. The next chapter brings us back to your toolbox and shows how to pick the best story idea for your audience.

SUMMARY

Start with Your Audience, Not with the Story

See the checklists in the back of the book.

- Stories start with your audience, not the idea. Your audience should feel like you are sitting across from each other having a conversation.
- Create a persona(s) for your audience. There may be a few in each audience. This includes demographics, hobbies, and a typical day-in-the-life. The persona represents your audience and gives an idea of who you are speaking to.
- Define the desired outcomes for what you want your audience to know, feel, think, or do.
- Define your audience's mindset and any potential obstacles in the desired outcomes.

Bofta Yimam

*Emmy and Edward R. Murrow Award-Winning Television
Correspondent, International Speaker, and Entrepreneur*

What role does video play in your stories?

Video is a central part of every story I tell as a broadcast journalist. When video is weaved in effectively with strong writing, it pulls the viewer in and helps tell a more compelling story. I have always thought of my photographer as my partner in this visual storytelling. One of the things that we discuss is, "What are the elements we have for this piece?" Elements could be sound bites, photographs, or "B-roll" of a specific scene that highlights something or someone in the story.

The more elements I have to support the piece, the richer it tends to be. Elements help tell a fuller story. They also can help connect to the emotions of the story. A key moment in the interview might be matched with a tight video shot. A sequence of shots can be matched to the length of a sentence to create cadence.

How do you work with the emotions in a story?

The focus is always on why people should care about the story. What is it that would make someone hear the beginning of this story while in the kitchen, leave their coffee on the counter, and walk over to the TV to watch? This is where emotions and compelling writing can be used to spark or continue interest in the piece through the interview, video, sound bites, and/or natural sound.

In the interview, my job is to find the truth—but humanizing a story is often how the audience stays engaged. This may involve going deeper with a specific interviewee, like asking the tough questions that the public wants the answers to, pinpointing where the interviewee was at a specific moment of time, how they felt in the experience, what other factors may have played a role, and why it all matters.

83

The interviewee is oftentimes letting you into the worst or best moment of their life, or someplace in between. It's a skill to be able to weave in the range of emotions of these moments alongside the appropriate elements and context to help the audience connect and digest the story easily. This requires discerning the best sound bites and video clips to help bring a story alive. We have to do this effectively and efficiently since most daily news pieces are no longer than one minute and thirty seconds! It's so important to think about, *What can we add or remove to help keep the heart and focus of this story?*

I've always thought that great journalism teaches people things— whether it's a new vaccine being developed or an experience someone went through. Experiences can be wide and varying—a reminder about the goodness of human beings, how someone turned a tragedy into something beautiful, or how someone showed their resilience in a unique way. We are all humans experiencing emotions and wanting to connect and relate to others. Storytelling helps us showcase that beautifully.

SIX

Select an Idea for Your Story

"Two kids were fighting over who would get the last orange. After arguing in circles without progress, they decided to split it in half. One child took half the orange, ate it, and threw the peel away. The other child took the other half of the orange, separated the peel from the fruit, and threw the orange away, using the peel to bake a cake."

Ten years ago, I was launching a leadership development course on negotiations. I asked two companies to facilitate a pilot training session so I could choose the one that was the best fit. Both companies started their session with a version of this story—struggling over an orange. It comes from *Getting to Yes*, a popular negotiations book by Roger Fisher and William Ury. That specific example is provided as a brief metaphor of how negotiation communications can break down.

I was confused when each company used this example. Kids argue over the same thing all the time. But orange segments versus an orange peel? How often does a kid want orange zest for baking? There is no tension or relatability. The stakes aren't high—it's just an orange. Help us connect with either kid—or both—on why the orange was so important to them. Help us feel the weight of the orange in their hand, or smell the waves of citrus rise through the air as they struggled. Let us feel the frustration of either child not feeling heard. Connect us to the anger felt when both children realized they could have had 100 percent of what they wanted but missed out due to communication.

It's the wrong story to open a class for a business audience who comes with the mindset that negotiating is a difficult topic riddled with mistakes. There is no emotional engagement or connection to the story. It fails to leverage the Five Factory Settings of the Brain. The story only reinforces the belief that negotiations are hard to learn.

The *Getting to Yes* book includes many different stories on the nuances of negotiations, but both companies automatically grabbed this one to open and set the tone. Each time, it fell flat. These companies had a great depth of experience in business and government negotiations, rich with examples for a meaningful and relevant opening.

They defaulted to existing stories—the same thing as impulsively buying something at the cash register. The problem with an impulse buy is that it isn't a necessity and often distracts you from remembering what you need. It's easier to look for something that already exists than to figure out and create what would be most helpful. Each time you use an existing story or metaphor without modification, you risk that story not working for your audience. It may feel easier and require less work, but you don't gain anything by using it.

How many times have you heard the phrase "Culture eats strategy for breakfast"? I groan every time I see it in a presentation, article, or business book. It's overused and signals the brain to slide into lazy mode because we've heard it so many times before. Most people don't remember it was included a few minutes later because it's so common. Yet people use this because it's there and it's easy. Don't waste your audience's attention by sending their brain into lazy mode.

One of my friends told me, "I often try to think of the exact right business phrases when I am speaking. Other times I am myself." My advice to her? Be unique. Don't try to find the overused, unmemorable businesses phrases or stories. No one has ever said, "I wish that presentation had more business lingo." Tell the story only you can tell. Use novel examples and details. You won't be memorable if you use common phrases. You will when you make your stories personal by sharing your perspective.

> No one has ever said, "I wish that presentation had more business lingo."

Don't tell a story just because it's sitting there like an impulse buy. Your choice of a story shouldn't be because you heard someone else tell it. Pick an idea for a story because you feel something toward it or you see how to create a connection for your audience. Even when it's a story you have heard elsewhere—you need to have some excitement for or interest in the story. That excitement will help you build the idea or outcome for your audience.

FOLLOW THE FEELING

Do you know the excitement you feel when picking a bottle of wine, an ice cream flavor, or a menu item at a restaurant? The curiosity you notice as you select a book to read. The "I want to see that!" feeling after watching a movie trailer. The eagerness of picking out a new pair of sneakers or set of golf clubs. It's a twinge of interest or the perfect mix of excitement and anticipation. The feelings you experience in those moments are exactly what you're looking for when you are choosing a story idea—even if the story will make others uncomfortable. You want to feel an interest for the story you're about to tell.

Great stories exchange energy between the storyteller and the audience. Especially when we apply the techniques to leverage the Five Factory Settings. That energy connects your excitement in telling the story to your audience's experience. If you don't feel something, creating the story will feel harder, forced, and flat. Think of people who had a lot of enthusiasm around a story they were telling. That energy was contagious and shared with the audience. You could feel their excitement. Authenticity shines through, and the audience often responds with an increase in oxytocin and empathy. You can't fake that interest.

SELECTING AN IDEA FOR A STORY

We return to the center of the model to the toolbox of potential story ideas you created earlier. Scan your list of ideas. For each one, ask yourself, "Does this idea . . ."

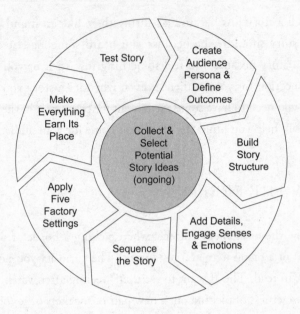

- Have points or a theme that align with the outcome I want for my audience?
- Connect to a pain point or aspiration of the audience?
- Help the audience feel a part of a group or different from a group?
- Help tell a story that makes my audience feel good or uncomfortable?
- Work as a metaphor for my desired outcome?
- Combine with another idea to create a takeaway that reinforces the desired outcome?
- Change if told from a different perspective?
- Make me feel any energy or excitement to share it?
- Prompt new story ideas?

You're looking for two things: Can you see a connection to the desired outcome for your audience? Do you feel energy or excitement around the idea?

Sometimes it can be hard to see what story can be made from an idea. Uncover options by experimenting with the different perspectives from which the story can be told. The story about Walt failing his exam would have a different focus if told from the perspective of Dottie, as she describes feeling invisible in the rooms she cleans.

Often, the very act of scanning the list of ideas will prompt a brand-new idea. This may include combining two of the ideas, like I did with Walt and Maria. A fresh idea may emerge as the right one for your story. As I scan my list, I frequently think of a new idea not in my toolbox and add it for future stories.

It's OK if you're still unsure what the story looks like at this point. Think of it as collecting ingredients to make a recipe. You're searching for ingredients to figure out the various recipes you can make with them. Some ingredients will be fresh, and you want to use them before they go bad. Some ingredients may leave you saying, "Eh, I'm not feeling this today." Like a recipe, a great story is made from the way you combine the details to result in the desired outcomes. Look through your ideas to see which ones have enough of the right ingredients to shape into the perfect story for your audience.

Back in the Elevator . . .

I was with Maria the day she dropped her phone down the elevator shaft. I told her, "I am going to do something with this story, but I don't know what yet." I knew there was an idea, but I wasn't sure how to use it. It intrigued me, and I added it to my toolkit.

A few weeks later, I wrote the story, but something was missing. It built tension, but the idea didn't feel strong enough. It wasn't until I read the article about Walt Bettinger in the *New York Times* that it clicked. Individually the stories are both interesting. Combined, they create these unexpected, heart-sinking moments that result in a stronger takeaway. They help you feel like you are Maria or Walt—or Dottie or Ray.

If I hadn't found the story of Walt Bettinger, I would have shelved Maria's story until I figured it out. Sometimes you get inspired by an idea, but it needs more work to turn into the right story. Stories need to breathe. I often start with an idea and realize it doesn't work or needs more time. You may dump your idea and go back into the toolkit a few times until you have a story that feels meaningful.

I'd love to say I planned to use Walt and Maria's story for the TED Talk all along. I had written it several years before and was looking for a different one to tell. I kept finding stories that worked for the Darren persona but ignored Grace's, or stories that didn't make the points I wanted for the audience about storytelling and leadership. They didn't work, and I could feel it. I reviewed my personas, desired outcomes, and list of ideas, and it became clear this was the right story for both personas.

Grace and Darren have their mobile phones as an appendage and would be lost without them. The thought of their phone falling down an elevator shaft would make them uncomfortable. Walt's story in a university setting was relatable for both Grace and Darren. When I tested the story the first time, I felt the excitement of the combined idea. The story clicked into place as I worked on how to share my perspective.

Selecting an idea can feel uncomfortable. Tension grows when you don't know what story you will tell and you face a deadline. That discomfort is normal and part of the process. Your brain is on alert and looking for the story. This is why collecting ideas is an ongoing practice and separate from the storytelling process. Scanning the already gathered list of ideas gives a starting point that doesn't rely on creating from a blank sheet of paper.

Discomfort is a signal to trust the process. It's an indicator that you haven't found the right idea to share—yet. Once you see an idea that sparks your interest, that feeling will shift. Stories aren't waiting fully formed on a shelf. The process of finding an idea often creates doubt, with your inner voice raising objections. These mental protests are common.

YOUR TOPIC ISN'T BORING ... AND OTHER STORYTELLING EXCUSES THAT ARE WRONG

When it comes time to pick an idea for a story, excuses begin emerging, protesting why a story shouldn't be told. Most are wrong. They're a signal of being afraid of telling a story that falls flat. The storytelling process can be applied to each context to create engaging stories.

My Topic Is Boring

"I have to talk about boring topics—there just aren't ways to tell an interesting story about my topic."

I hear this frequently, and each time I think, *Challenge accepted!* It doesn't matter if you are talking about policies, products, data, or regulations, there is always a way to tell an interesting story. Stories are about people, situations, and problems. Within those are details you can dig into. Share specific stories of the hopes, dreams, aspirations, or fears of an individual's experience. Recount the problems you solve and describe the transformations and shifts made. The opportunities for interesting stories are endless. It's just a matter of digging into details that help you build the outcome desired for your audience. A great example of this comes from Tennant, an industrial cleaning supply company that tells stories about the people who use their products.

Tennant sells cleaning supplies to schools. While necessary, they're hardly sexy to market. Tennant launched the "Custodians Are Key" campaign to tell the stories of those who use their products and rarely get recognition. School administrators submitted nominations, and the winning custodian and school received money.

The first year of the program, the winner was Kris Kantor of Hayes Elementary School in Lakewood, Ohio. He found the cleaning products worked so well that he had more time to connect with students and faculty. Not only was Kris fastidious about organization and cleanliness, but he was also devoted to the students, teachers, and staff. Kris knew the names of all 300-plus people at the school. He created "Kids with Kantor" to teach kids how to build things like birdhouses, decorative boxes, and toy helicopters during lunch. Kris wasn't just teaching proper tool use and safety; the kids learned teamwork and respect.

The first year of the contest, there were over 2,000 nominees. These nominated stories added depth to Tennant's products and reinforced their values: creating a clean and safe environment for everyone to thrive.

Before the contest, school administrators wouldn't have been able to name a single Tennant product, despite owning the budget. Tennant called administrators of participating schools to thank them, and 30 percent of these calls turned into sales. "Custodians are Key" became an annual contest with nominations steadily increasing. Not only has Tennant created goodwill, but they also have endless stories to share.

If you feel you have a boring topic, dig into the details. Consider the story from different perspectives. Tell the story of one person, one product, or one problem. Help engage your audience's senses and emotions surrounding that one person or circumstance. There is always an angle that can be brought to a story that helps people connect with it differently.

The Skeptical Leadership Team

Morgan was hired to be a disruptor, helping her company embrace a new data-informed way of thinking and working. As the head of marketing for a furniture company, she had a new vision and strategy for their products and services. By custom designing furniture to fit awkward home layouts, the company could create a VIP experience.

Morgan was challenged by a few skeptics on the leadership team who felt they already knew what customers would buy. Once a week Morgan was interrupted with, "That isn't how we do things." Most had been with the company twenty years. As the newest member of the leadership team, she grappled to establish trust.

Morgan and I began working together when the CEO asked her to present the strategy at a company-wide meeting. She thought employees would be excited about her vision, but she struggled with the complacency and apathy of the leadership team. She needed alignment from both employees and leadership to be successful but felt stuck communicating to an audience of different mindsets.

As we worked through the two personas, we recognized over 90 percent of the audience would be employees. I told Morgan to focus her story on them to create a groundswell of enthusiasm and interest in the strategy. The leadership team would likely need different messaging. Her energy should go to the employees, not the 10 percent of outliers.

Morgan told the story of three different clients going through the VIP experience, walking through employee interactions for each step of the process. After the talk, a long line of employees formed to ask her questions.

At the next leadership meeting, a peer asked Morgan a question about the strategy. Before she could reply, another leadership team member responded. She had always been the one describing the strategy—now there were other supporting voices. After watching employees gain interest, leadership team members wanted to help Morgan in the path to new growth without being left behind.

Sometimes a story results in an immediate shift. Other times you are planting seeds of ideas that can be built upon. Skeptics are often in your audience, and it can be helpful to think of your audience as a bell curve. What majority are you speaking to in your story? Skeptics may fall outside of the majority. Your energy should go toward where you can have the greatest impact.

I Don't Have Time to Present a Story

As you think about telling a story, you may hear your inner voice whisper, *What are you doing? You don't have time to tell a story.* The length of a story doesn't determine if it's good; the structure and immersion of the audience do. It's more challenging to tell a lengthy story that engages and holds the listener's attention than it is to tell a shorter, impactful story. But most short stories require work to make them tight and impactful.

Many people feel they don't have time to tell a story because they don't know how to structure and tell a compelling and concise story. They tell stories with details meaningful to themselves but irrelevant to the audience. The listener loses interest as the stories ramble and include unnecessary details.

Upcoming chapters cover how to build an impactful story structure. Once you learn it, experiment with creating short, medium, and long versions of your stories. Expand or collapse the descriptions of the details, senses, and emotions along the story structure. Longer versions include more details that move the story forward, share insights about characters, or engage the brain. Shorter versions give just enough information to create the desired outcome for what you want the audience to know, think, do, or feel. I told the medium version of Maria dropping the phone down an elevator shaft. I removed pieces that were entertaining but could save time and not sacrifice the impact of the story.

Leaders Don't Need to Tell Stories

Victor had a habit of sucking all the air out of the room when speaking to employees. As the CEO, he loved talking with them, but he never organized his thoughts. He would ramble for thirty minutes. Employees would drift off and make mental grocery lists.

A member of his leadership team suggested he plan a few points and customer stories to share in advance. Victor refused, not wanting to waste time planning. He felt employees would listen to anything he had to say. He failed to recognize that more time was lost in employees tuning out than would be spent in preparation.

Leaders often think they're exempt from telling stories. They believe this myth that once you reach a certain level, people are required to listen to you. But we've all sat through enough boring leadership presentations to know that isn't true. People will check out when a message is incoherent, irrelevant, or rambling.

| Stories become talking points that are repeated. |

Stories extend your leadership. They not only demonstrate what you value and encourage, they get discussed when you aren't there. Stories become talking points that are repeated. They give oxygen to employees and can inspire thinking and action.

I Can't Tell a Story; I Must Present Data

If you're presenting data, a story can prevent misinterpretation and guide the audience to a common understanding. Data isn't a reason to avoid telling a story; it should be a consideration for telling one. Finding an idea for a data story often involves identifying the smallest story you can tell from the data set—like the story of one person. Once people connect to the story of that person, they will better understand the scale of the data. You often see this done with nonprofits. The chapter "Storytelling with Data" walks through how to find an idea and tell a story with data in detail.

Picking an idea for your story helps you begin to see how you will create the desired outcome for your persona. While tempting to think of excuses for why a story might not work in your circumstances, don't talk yourself out of telling one. I find the challenge isn't that people tell the wrong stories for their setting, it's that they don't tell *enough* stories. Focus on finding the idea you're most excited about sharing with your audience. Dig into the details to uncover what is interesting about your topic.

At some point when choosing an idea, you will consider, *Do I have to tell a personal story?* Every story is personal, even if you are telling someone else's story. People often have misconceptions around sharing personal stories. They even wonder if they should make up stories. That is what we will explore next.

SUMMARY

Select an Idea for Your Story

See the checklists in the back of the book.

- Follow the feeling: when picking an idea, take note of those you have excitement or interest to share.
- Great stories are an exchange of energy between the storyteller and the audience.
- Selecting an idea: Look through your toolkit of ideas. Select the one that helps you achieve the desired outcome: what you want your audience to know, think, feel or do differently.
- Reviewing your toolkit of ideas often triggers new ideas for a story.
- Consider combining ideas or telling them from different perspectives for additional options.
- Trust the process, even when it feels uncomfortable. Discomfort is an indicator that you haven't found the right idea to share yet.
- If you feel your topic is boring, dig into the details to learn more about the people, situations, and specifics involved.
- Don't focus on the skeptics. Keep your persona in mind. Your audience may have a mix of your personas and skeptics.
- Great stories don't have to be lengthy. Stories become lengthy and drag when they lack structure.
- Leaders aren't exempt from storytelling. Stories can extend your leadership, creating discussion when you aren't around.
- Storytelling and data are a powerful combination. Stories help the data become more understandable.

Stephanie Stuckey

CEO of Stuckey's Corporation

You have created an impressive profit for Stuckey's through story-telling. Do you remember the first story you told?

The first story that really took off happened at my lowest point, a few months after acquiring the company. I pulled over at an old Stuckey's that looked so bad. It was this greasy-looking, terrible gas station with the most deplorable bathrooms. It would have horrified my grandfather to see what had happened to a beautiful store that was once an invit-ing and welcoming oasis on the Interstate. While we don't currently own or operate the stores, we do sell our pecan log rolls, nuts, and candy treats in them.

Before that moment, I had tried to post very upbeat, positive stories about our brand's comeback. This day, I put up a picture of the store. I said something like, "I am driving the backroads of Alabama in search of a lost Stuckey's. Like this country, our brand has seen better days. But I am determined to do everything I can to help revive both."

I put that on LinkedIn. Prior to that, I had been getting maybe twenty likes on my posts from friends and family. That post completely took off. Within a couple of days, it had a quarter of a million views, thousands of hits, and hundreds of personal comments.

That is when I realized that, to really connect with people, you have to be authentic. The only way you can be authentic is to be vulnerable. There is only one path to authenticity, and it is going through vulnerability.

Have you always told stories—even before buying back your family's business?

I'm a Southerner. I grew up sitting on the front porch after church telling stories. It's in our DNA. I just know we would go to church, have a big Sunday supper, and sit around and talk. Meals were a time to share stories. I've always been entertained by stories.

I jot down inspiration in two ways. My home computer has a running page for ideas of social media posts called "That would make a great post!" If I am away from my computer, I have a note on my iPhone where I have a whole page of social media ideas. There are literally 50–75 different post ideas in each of those formats. Now that I do video content, I do the same thing. I will shoot short video and save it in drafts. When I have a day crammed with work and don't have time to shoot any video content, I'll pull something up from my drafts.

Which stories resonate most?

I think the stories about road trips because they transcend a lot of demographics. Any age, ethnicity, or gender can relate to road trips. Those are the fun ones. I have a "brand diamond." It's an illustration that looks like a diamond with the seven facets I talk about in my posts. I try to hit on at least one of them every time I tell a story. They include road trips, families, Americana, pecans, nostalgia, and Southern hospitality. You have to find the commonalities that are going to help people relate to you.

SEVEN

Do I Have to Tell a Personal Story?

I've written and told over 100 stories in articles and keynotes. Without fail, the ones that include a personal story generate the most interaction and connection. It doesn't matter if the topic is a positive moment or a failure with a difficult lesson—they make me relatable and approachable. New clients often reference these stories in our first meeting. They describe hearing the story several months prior in a keynote or reading it in a blog post and say, "I feel like I already know you from this story!"

As much as I use storytelling, I don't share private stories. I have a high privacy barrier. Rarely will I share a story about my family unless it is focused on me or my experience. However, I am quite comfortable sharing a story about my failures and mistakes because they don't cross a personal boundary. I view them as teachable moments that help to build a specific idea for the audience.

Each time I share a personal story, I am positively overwhelmed by the response. I receive emails, cards, and messages from the audience that describe how my story resonated with them. Many share stories and photos in return. Personal stories help create a sense of connection far more quickly than any information or facts I could have given instead.

As you begin to think about how you'll connect with your audience, you may wonder, *Do I have to tell a personal story?* Storytelling by nature is vulnerable. Telling a story about yourself can amplify that feeling. The stakes somehow feel higher when sharing something personal. In many environments and regions, telling a personal story can feel like you are inappropriately boasting or bragging. I find there is a wide continuum for what is considered "personal," ranging from sharing your perspective to oversharing or revealing private details.

"PERSONAL" DOESN'T MEAN "PRIVATE"

Choosing to tell a personal story doesn't mean you have to share private details. Boundaries are important in storytelling, and each person gets to decide their own. What may feel private to one person may be completely comfortable to another. You determine what is private and not shared.

A personal story doesn't require sharing anything revealing. Anytime you share a story, tell the version only you can tell. Give your perspective—even when you're telling a story about someone else. Private details aren't required to share your personal connection to something. Your audience will relate and respond to your perspective.

As you experiment with storytelling, you may find a stronger audience response when you share a story about yourself. Think back to a moment when someone told a story that gave insight into who they are as a person. You likely felt a sense of connection and deeper understanding. Stories reinforce what we value and care about on a personal level. Sharing personal stories can make your audience feel as though you're saying, "I trust you enough to share this with you." They reciprocate your gesture with increased trust and empathy toward you.

Personal Stories Don't Make You Weak

Lina reached out to me for help with a presentation for an annual company all-hands meeting. As the head of research and development in an engineering company, she was trying to figure out the right story to help the company embrace the strategy for the coming year. As we talked about the desired outcomes, she said, "I just have one requirement: I don't want to tell a personal story. I'm the only woman on a leadership team of men who are fifteen years older than me. I have young children. Their kids are out of the house, and I gather they weren't hands-on parents when they were young. I already feel judged as I try to balance my family with work. I don't want to share a story about myself or my family and give them a reason to view me as weak."

Have you ever wondered, *Will telling a personal story make me look weak?* Occasionally, these are indications that the topic is private and something you don't want to share, like Lina experienced. You're also sensing the vulnerability and discomfort that is often felt when sharing something personal. But what you feel internally is different from what people experience. Sharing a personal story usually results in the audience feeling you are self-aware and authentic, not that you're weak. Often, their empathy toward you grows, and they may even feel a part of the same in-group as they relate to your story and experiences.

It May Feel Uncomfortable to Tell a Story About Yourself

Ryan was a CEO of a Fortune 500 finance company and was bringing his team together for the first time in a year. The business was struggling, and the team needed to work through conflict and set a new strategy. As Ryan and I reviewed the agenda and format of the workshop, I pointed out where I wanted him to open with a personal story. I told him it didn't have to be revealing or private, but he needed to share something to make him relatable, approachable, and set the tone for the meeting.

I hadn't finished saying the sentence, "I want you to share a personal story . . ." before Ryan started squirming. "I don't want to make this about me," he said. "Telling a personal story could feel either like I'm oversharing or I'm bragging."

"I get it," I replied. "I don't want you to share anything that feels revealing. The goal is to make you more approachable and demonstrate your trust in the team. If you start by sharing something personal, they'll understand you better and be more open to the difficult conversations we need to have."

Ryan wasn't immediately sold and told me he would think about it. After he welcomed the group on the day of the session, he took a long pause. Then he told the group his father was disabled. His voice rippled with emotion as he described the challenges his father faced and the impact his disability had on Ryan's life, decisions, and leadership.

People learned more about Ryan in that three-minute story than they had learned over the past year. The energy notably shifted as the team responded to his authenticity. Ryan's story also set a tone. Others began sharing stories. Trust increased and defensiveness decreased across the team. They were able to have difficult conversations to address their challenges.

Telling stories about yourself can feel exposing and uncomfortable. They feel like you're standing center stage in a spotlight saying, "Me, me, me, meeeeeeeee!" Yet thoughtfully shared personal stories create the greatest connection and trust.

Vulnerability is key in a great story—whether you tell one about yourself or someone else. It's why there is a whole chapter dedicated to it later in this book. When you tell stories about yourself, that feeling is amplified. You often experience the emotions again when telling the story. It's tempting to avoid it altogether. Yet, this is how you create the greatest connection and meaning with your audience.

TELLING OTHER PEOPLE'S STORIES IS STILL PERSONAL

Telling stories about other people can still have a personal touch when you bring your perspective, insights, and energy to them. Your story may be about someone else, but it becomes personal as you share your perspective. Even if a story has been told before, it hasn't been told by *you*. Make the story your own by helping the audience understand your perspective of the characters and events.

The opening and closing stories of my TED Talk are about other people told from my perspective. I highlight what stood out to me and what I took away from each. While they aren't stories about me, they are personal. You get a sense of what I value through the way I tell these stories.

Whenever deciding to tell a story about someone else that isn't already in the public domain, get their permission. If I want to tell a story about a friend or client, I make sure they're supportive of the story and validate any details they want removed, anonymized, or kept confidential. I never want to surprise someone or reveal unwanted information.

Once you have the approval to tell someone else's story, focus on making it your own by adding your perspective and thoughts. You may want to ask yourself a few questions first: *Why does the story resonate with you and make you want to share it with others? How do you connect with the story? How do you want to connect your audience to this story?* As you think about the idea you want to build for your audience, think about how you can incorporate your perspective. Help the audience understand why you are sharing this story.

Considerations for Telling Someone Else's Story

Great stories help the audience feel like they are hearing, seeing, feeling, and experiencing the events. When telling someone else's story, people often focus on getting the events of the story right and forget to engage the senses and emotions. Each story should help the audience gain the feeling of firsthand experience.

Ask yourself, *What would I be doing if I were in this story? What would I be feeling? How would I change throughout the story? Where would I struggle? What would I realize?* When you're telling someone else's story, your risk is not including enough details or specificity that make the story meaningful for your audience. This includes explaining your connection to or realizations about the story so your audience knows why you're telling it in the first place.

Considerations for Telling Your Story

Sharing personal stories may feel more straightforward. We often tell these with a different energy, easily describing the details and emotions we experienced firsthand. The challenge is in figuring out which details are relevant. There may be pieces of the story that were important to you but not as meaningful for the audience. Leave yourself enough time to thoughtfully work through the storytelling process to figure out the right details to share. We'll talk about how to do this in the coming chapters.

CAN I MAKE UP STORIES?

At some point you will wonder, *Can I make up a story?*

No.

Not unless you are a novelist, a screenwriter, or creating a work of fiction.

Your audience only connects to your desired outcome when they believe your story and trust you as the storyteller. The moment you start making up stories, you can guarantee you'll be perceived as manipulative and untrustworthy. Think of politicians or journalists that you feel intentionally tell misleading or manipulated statements or stories. Your opinion of them tanks, and you doubt anything they say going forward.

There are a few exceptions. It's always acceptable to change names or personal identifying information. When I share stories about a client, I change personal information, personal descriptions, company names, and industries for anonymity. But I don't change plot points. You can swap minor details. An event taking place on a Thursday instead of a Tuesday doesn't change the plot.

"Imagine when . . ." stories are made-up accounts about a vision for the future. Team retreats often include a "Close your eyes and imagine it is a year from now . . ." prompt. These stories help us imagine the experience of something significant being realized or changed. Your goal is to help guide the audience to imagine what the experience could be like through the made-up story. The key is to be clear about your intent—why you are doing this, and what you are trying to achieve.

Some stories may describe a typical experience of employees or customers. You may want to combine the experience of a few people into one in the story to fill in minor details, like dialogue or descriptions. These stories aren't made up—they tell real events and experiences. One of my clients was telling a story about someone she coached. She remembered the main events of the story, but over the years, some of the dialogue slipped away. She combined dialogue from conversations with a few different people in identical circumstances to fill in the gaps in the story—without changing the facts or plot.

If you make up a story, particularly about a product, service, or cause, it can flop terribly and reek of manipulation. Trust is lost when audiences sniff out manipulative, made-up stories (and trust me, they *will* sniff them out). There are so many rich ideas and examples around you; don't make up or mislead parts of a story. Once you choose the idea, use the structure and process to build a meaningful story for your audience.

Back in the Elevator . . .

Once I chose the story about Maria and Walt for my TED Talk, I focused on how I could make it personal. I asked myself, *Why am I the right one to tell this story? What do I bring to this story?* I recognized the story was personal from the idea I built and how I told it.

I chose to combine Maria's story with Walt's to connect the audience to the importance of making people feel seen, especially as a leader. Through the story, you consider how you might respond in either situation.

The Five Factory Settings are engaged throughout the story. Tension is built and assumptions are challenged as Walt's exam paper is blank when turned over and Maria learns she can get her phone back for an expensive fee. I engage the senses through specific words and gestures. Both stories intentionally take you through a moment of discomfort to help the audience feel part of an in-group that wants people to feel seen. While I don't explicitly say "I think" or "I feel," my perspective is clear throughout the story. I almost become a character through my personal delivery.

WEDDING TOASTS AND EULOGIES

Wedding toasts and eulogies are the most personal stories we will ever share. They create connection, flood you with emotion, and celebrate life. Specific considerations help identify the best story to honor loved ones for these moments.

Eulogies

My friend Tonya called me with the news she had been dreading—her dear friend Kelly had passed away after a long bout with brain cancer. Kelly was the person in town everyone seemed to know. She was an athletic trainer, sat on the board of her local art museum, and volunteered with multiple charities. Her family planned to hold the memorial service at the museum, expecting more than two hundred people to attend. They asked Tonya to provide a eulogy for Kelly. She couldn't say no. Yet anytime she spoke in public, she became so nervous that her face and neck ended up covered in splotchy red patches. She had no idea what to say, especially in front of such a large audience.

I asked Tonya to tell me a memory that was "so Kelly," something she did that others wouldn't necessarily think to do, but Kelly wouldn't have it any other way. Tonya started laughing and described a time she and her husband had to go out of town unexpectedly because his father was ill. They left so suddenly that she had to text Kelly from the road to ask her to bring in their mail each day. After a week away, they came home to fresh flowers and cookies on their table with a note from Kelly. Their fridge was stocked with roasted chicken, green beans, and mashed potatoes. She'd even cleaned their kitchen and left washed towels in a neat stack next to the mail.

As she shared the story, Tonya started laughing at the memory of it. "The kitchen looked better than when I've cleaned it. I never have fresh flowers! That was *so* Kelly," Tonya remembered. "She was always thoughtful. She had a knack for paying attention to the details that made you feel so good."

I told her to start the eulogy there. It would give the guests a story about Kelly they didn't know and make them laugh. I promised Tonya that the moment she heard the first laugh, she would relax. Sure enough, chuckles rippled across the audience and heads nodded as Tonya described the plate of cookies and freshly washed towels. Tonya found herself smiling and was able to make it through the eulogy and honor Kelly's legacy.

Eulogies are the stories everyone dreads having to tell. Figuring out the right way to honor a person's life can weigh heavily on the best of storytellers. Navigating your emotions while giving the eulogy is even harder.

If you're giving a eulogy, focus on doing three things: honor and celebrate the person's life and legacy, help the audience learn more about the person, and share stories that the guests may not know. Focusing on these three desired outcomes makes it easier to identify stories to share. Some prompts to consider:

- What do you admire about this person?
- When did the person do something that was "so them"?
- What is your favorite thing about this person?
- What is the funniest situation you saw this person in?
- If you could relive a day with this person, what would it be?
- What is a story about this person many people wouldn't know?
- What was this person particular about—like food not touching on a plate?
- How did you meet this person?
- What holidays, vacations, or experiences did you share with the person?
- What's a funny quirk about this person, like *always* taking a photo with a finger in the frame?

A eulogy often includes different stories that help the audience learn more about the person. While there is no wrong way to give a eulogy, I suggest opening with a story that embodies the person—something that is "so them." When you share something that is a clear illustration of who the person was, the audience will laugh. These first laughs help you to relax and make it easier to continue the speech. From there, you can establish your relationship with the person, if not already done through the opening story. The next section can celebrate the person through highlighting personal or professional events and achievements. These often include where the person lived, significant relationships in their life, hobbies and groups they were a part of, and work accomplishments. The closing can touch on what the person meant to you, what you have learned from them and are carrying forward.

You may choose to include several small stories throughout each section to punctuate characteristics of the loved one. Or you may weave in a few strategically placed stories as you recount their life and impact. Whatever you choose, plan your stories in advance of delivering the eulogy. Avoid rambling by identifying the stories you want to tell and the key points you want to share. This will make it easier to navigate your emotions and celebrate the loved one with your audience. Later chapters share how to structure and build your stories.

Wedding or Engagement Toasts

Wedding toasts often cover many of the same things that eulogies do, but the tone is different. While eulogies look backward, wedding toasts tend to focus on who the couple is in that moment, their journey to the moment, and their future.

Like a eulogy, a wedding toast is a chance for the audience to learn more about the couple and hear stories that are "so them." Your goal is to connect the audience to the love and support felt for the couple in about three minutes. Avoid dropping in random stories or inside jokes that others won't understand.

Wedding toasts typically include your connection with the couple, their unique qualities, what they mean to you, and a celebration and wish for their future. While eulogies are often made up of many stories, a toast usually includes one or two. Your story may even introduce an overall theme or idea that you refer to in the closing as you offer a wish for their future.

Here are a few prompts to consider for toasts:

- When did you meet the couple?
- What is your first memory of them individually or as a couple?
- When did you know they were meant to be?
- What is an example that demonstrates who they are as a couple?
- What was the behind-the-scenes story of their engagement that most guests wouldn't know?
- How have you seen them grow as a couple?
- What have you learned from the couple?
- Do you have a specific theme for the toast like "love" or "happiness"? If so, what is a story about the couple that embodies the theme?

The audience for a toast is already engaged. The love hormone, oxytocin, is flowing and there is a lot of excitement and support in the room. This makes your job as a storyteller easier. Your audience is already on your side, ready to laugh, cheer, and feel "all the feels" with a heartfelt story or two about the couple. A story can work at any part of the toast: as part of the opening and as you establish your connection to the couple; in the middle, connected to an overall theme or tidbit about the couple; or at the closing, to end the toast on an emotional note. Like with eulogies, plan ahead to know the stories you want to tell and the key points you want to share.

Stories told in eulogies and toasts follow the same development steps in other stories: What do you want your audience to think or feel after the eulogy or toast? Which idea are you most interested to tell? In the coming chapters, you'll learn how to follow the storytelling model to build out your story in a compelling way that engages the senses and emotions. You'll be able to make your personal stories even more vivid with your perspective.

JOB INTERVIEWS

Job interviews are opportunities to share personal stories that build an understanding of you in the interviewer's mind, shaping their assumptions and first impressions. The interviewer filters their understanding of you through their knowledge and experiences. Stories can help create the understanding you'd like the interviewer to come away with.

Remember, storytelling results in connection, trust, and empathy. Whether you're interviewing for a new company or a different department within your existing company, you are a member of both in- and out-groups. Through a story, you create an in-group feeling for the hiring manager to view you as "just like them" as you describe your similar experiences, values, or aspirations. Your stories can also create an out-group feeling as you highlight the different knowledge and experience you bring. These help the hiring manager see where your diverse thinking and approaches would complement the team.

When you hear a candidate is "not a good culture fit," it's often because the manager views them as a member of an out-group. The candidate failed to connect the dots for the manager to understand how their experience would complement and not compete with the team. Telling stories that intentionally create the experience of in- and out-groups helps influence the understanding of how you would contribute to the role, team, and culture. A great story can be the differentiator for an interviewer feeling a connection and preference for one candidate over another.

I recommend three steps to prepare stories for interviews. First, define three words or phrases that describe you at your best. These should be characteristics you want the interviewer to come away thinking about you. For example, if asked, "Tell me about yourself," I might say, "You can think of me as a tour guide of storytelling. I take you to new destinations of communicating—teaching you along the way." Or I may answer, "I am a leadership whisperer, nudging leaders toward what they need to do and helping them understand why."

Be specific when defining these words or phrases. If you're going to use a common term like "conscientious," have a vivid, detailed description of what that uniquely looks like for you. Defining these words enables you to work them into the conversation and follow-up thank you messages. They act like themes, and anchor what the interviewer remembers and understands from their time with you.

Second, think of your interviewer's persona. Tailor your message and stories to them. Use the questions below to plan for each interview:

- What do you know about the interviewer?
- What do you want the interviewer to know about you?
- Why are you the right one for the role (in-group)?
- What do you uniquely bring to this role or organization (out-group)?
- What assumptions might the interviewer have about you?

Third, interviews are rich with "Tell me about a time . . ." questions. There are dozens of possible questions that interviewers may ask to understand your values, technical expertise, and communication, learning, and leadership styles. They often include variations of:

- Tell me about a time you faced conflict with a co-worker or team.
- Describe a time you made a mistake.
- Give an example of a time you demonstrated leadership skills.

- What is an example of when you had to reset expectations with a client?
- When did you have to think on your feet?
- Share a problem you have solved.
- How have you navigated a challenge?

Build a toolkit of possible stories for "Tell me about a time . . ." questions. Identify different examples that are relevant to the role you seek. Outline each story by writing out a sentence or two for each of the following:

1. **Challenge or conflict:** What was the problem or conflict you addressed? What was at stake? Why was this messy or hard? What would've happened if nothing had been done?
2. **Outcome:** What action did you take?
3. **Result:** What was the result of your actions?
4. **Learning:** What did you learn?

Your goal is to tell a story that engages the interviewer's brain, not just list roles and responsibilities. Build tension in your story by describing the conflict, what was at stake, what you set out to solve, and what would have happened if nothing was done. Finish the thought for the interviewer by telling what you learned, giving them the takeaway for the story.

It may be tempting to tell your interviewer a detailed story. However, what is interesting to you may not be to them. Think of your interview like a book. The first chapter is about your brand; each subsequent chapter includes stories about specific roles, projects, or experiences. Don't give away the entire book in each response. Provide enough information so they can understand your experience and the takeaway. Keep your stories under a minute and let the interviewer ask follow-up questions. Future chapters walk through how to incorporate metaphors, specific details and engage the interviewer's senses.

Stories are unique like snowflakes. They are personal, even when they're about someone else. Your stories don't have to reveal private information, but they do require your perspective. Tell the versions that only you can tell, especially for eulogies, toasts, and job interviews. As you select ideas, consider what you bring to the story and weave that throughout.

Great stories rely on a solid structure. These make the stories more succinct and easier to follow. That is where we go next, learning how to apply the four-part story structure to tell a compelling story for your audience.

SUMMARY

Do I Have to Tell a Personal Story?

See the checklists in the back of the book.

- *Personal* doesn't mean *private*. Personal stories don't require telling private information or oversharing. You decide your boundaries and what is private.
- Your audience will respond to the vulnerability of you sharing a personal story.
- All stories are personal, even if not your own. Bring your unique voice and perspective, even when telling someone else's story.
- Personal stories don't make you weak. They result in the audience gaining trust and empathy for you.
- Don't make up stories. Anytime you make up stories (apart from visioning), you risk your audience feeling manipulated and losing trust.
- Eulogies and toasts are often the most personal stories you will tell. Both help honor and celebrate a person and are an opportunity to share stories other guests may not know.
- Job interviews are opportunities to share stories that build an understanding of you in the interviewer's mind.

Drew Dudley

Keynote and TED Speaker: "Everyday Leadership," Bestselling Author

Your TED Talk went viral for a hilarious story about you introducing a future husband and wife with a lollipop in front of a crowd. How does it feel to be known as "The Lollipop Guy"?

I'm thrilled those six minutes of video are the catalyst for people to tell others they matter! However, it's important for me to point out that what happened in that story was an accident. It wasn't an intentional moment of leadership. That moment changed their lives, but I don't remember the interaction.

What do you want people to experience through your stories?

Storytelling is a tool to capture and keep people's attention. James Maskalyk, a physician from Doctors Without Borders, once told me, "The story is the basic unit of human understanding." I love that definition. I use stories to increase understanding of something—a process, perspective, or motivation.

Most ideas aren't new. I wrap them in Velcro, so they stick. I try to figure out how I can use a story to make people less afraid. Personal and organizational dysfunction comes from a fear of something being added or taken away without being ready. My stories offer insights on how to address those fears.

Sometimes I know the story I want to tell because it's engaging, teaches a lesson, or helps create a lighter moment. Other times I have an important belief, insight, or fact I want people to internalize. I ask myself, *What story can I tell that reflects this idea?*

When I was working on the lollipop story told for TED, I asked myself, *What does this lollipop story teach?* I realized people are afraid to call themselves a leader, viewing that as cocky or arrogant. The story demonstrates that they shouldn't feel that way.

I don't try to be motivating or inspiring when telling stories. As a speaker, I'm taking people's attention for a certain amount of time. I always go into it saying, *I want to be useful and share compelling ideas. How can this serve my audience?*

How did you become a great storyteller?

Much of my storytelling experience came from things I didn't realize had contributed. I read to my parents during long car rides as a kid, learning to add tension to a moment. Jerry Howarth and Tom Cheek showed me how to engage an audience through their commentating for the Toronto Blue Jays. They would describe the night air, the temperature, and the feeling of community, helping me feel like I was in the ballpark.

What advice would you give about storytelling?

Everyone should tell stories. Many don't know who needs to hear their stories, but your stories matter. I was driving through Idaho listening to an episode of *The Moth* podcast. A forest ranger was telling a story and said the phrase, "Grief is just love facing up to its oldest enemy." I had to pull over. My girlfriend had recently passed away. I hadn't cried until that moment. There was something about that story that I needed to hear. The speaker recorded it two years before, and she had no idea it would play on this day or how much it would mean to a stranger. So, tell your stories with the faith they will matter to someone.

PART THREE

The Conflict

Building the Story's Structure

EIGHT

Outline Your Story Structure

"The most important lesson I learned occurred while on vacation. This was two years ago—wait, maybe it was three years ago? No, no, it was two because three years ago I was in Peru, and this happened after *that trip. Anyhow, on the second day of the trip, I realized that I had misplaced my passport. Actually . . . it was the end of the first week. That's right, because when I went to buy a train ticket to the next city, I noticed my passport wasn't with my wallet like I thought it was . . ."*

Yasmin started her presentation with a story—or at least she tried to. After several moments of flip-flopping on the details and timing, she had yet to actually start the story. Her audience began tuning out as she struggled to recount details that weren't important.

Sound familiar?

Yasmin lost the audience before starting the plot of the story. She was so focused on remembering the timing of events that she didn't notice their attention drifting. This is a common mistake. People get hung up trying to recall specific details to accurately recount the story. The intent is good, but often most of those details aren't relevant to the audience. The storyteller needs a well-structured narrative that moves forward to build the desired outcome.

A great story isn't determined by length. It's created by building an idea that results in the audience's engagement and understanding. Choosing the idea gets you to the starting line. The work begins when you build the idea through a storytelling framework.

The story structure acts as the frame for major plot points and provides the scaffolding to layer details upon. The structure contributes two things: enabling the storyteller to map out a coherent story with ease, and helping the audience follow the story. You may not notice a story's structure, but you know when one is missing.

There are many different models for storytelling frameworks. You may have heard about *The Hero's Journey*, popularized by Joseph Campbell and used to create the original *Star Wars* films. Or Pixar's six-step storytelling model, leveraged from Kenn Adams, an improv comedian. These story structures are popular for a reason. They do a nice job of building tension to keep the audience's interest—especially when creating novels or screenplays.

I frequently hear people say they're challenged trying to use these frameworks to tell stories, especially in real-time. They get confused by the steps and struggle to fit their ideas into them. You aren't writing a novel, you're looking to tell a story that lands an idea in a meeting. You need a model that lets you build a story in an easy-to-understand way.

FOUR-PART STORY STRUCTURE

I created the four-part story structure based on the idea that stories have a beginning, middle, and end. However, I wanted something more dynamic, that also ensured the story leads to a desired outcome. The four-part structure incorporates the nuances of a great story: the context, conflict, outcome, and takeaway.

I had two goals when I created this structure. First, I want something simple and memorable. Second, I wanted to support the development of many different types of stories across a variety of contexts. I intentionally paired the four-part story structure with the circular step-by-step storytelling methodology to let you choose what you add—not force you into one format or type of story.

The four-part story structure works whether you have twenty minutes or two weeks to put a story together. It not only organizes your thoughts as the storyteller, but it also makes it easier for the audience to follow. I've even used it walking down the hall to a meeting to make sure I tell a focused story that lands desired key points.

Taking the idea you've selected for a story, write one or two summary sentences for each of the four sections below. These become the structure for your story.

1. What Is the Context?

Describe the setting of this story: who is involved, what is happening, and why should the audience care?

As I defined the context of the TED Talk story, I mapped out each story individually to figure out how they best fit together. Maria is at her office for a busy day and drops her phone down the elevator shaft. Walt Bettinger, CEO of Charles Schwab, had a 4.0 in college and was about to take his final exam.

A context sentence sets the scene and significant plot points in an intentionally high-level summary. It doesn't include every detail about Maria or Walt—or include every character.

2. What Is the Conflict?

Describe the moment where something happens and impacts the direction of the story. This is the fuel of your story—the conflict, tension, problem, or what is at stake. It's often the moment that sits between "before" and "after." You can point to it as the moment that things change.

The conflict of the TED Talk story: Maria learns her phone still works at the bottom of the elevator shaft, and includes her badge, credit cards, and driver's license. Ray tells her it will be expensive to retrieve. Walt is asked the name of the person who cleans the room and doesn't know the answer.

These sentences describe the conflict needing resolution in each story. They summarize what is at stake for Maria and Walt without specific details or dialogue.

3. What Is the Outcome?

Describe the result of the conflict. What happened to what was at stake? What action is taken, and what is the result?

The outcomes of the TED Talk story: Ray schedules the annual elevator inspection to retrieve Maria's phone for free; Walt fails his exam and realizes the leadership lesson he applies throughout his career.

These outcomes are high level, giving resolution to both Walt and Maria. Their path forward is implied, and there is a natural conclusion to both stories.

4. Takeaway: What Is the Overall Idea?

Summarize what you want your audience to know, think, feel, or do differently after the story. The takeaway lands the story idea for the audience. Try to write this as a short, pithy phrase. A succinct takeaway is easier for the audience to understand and recall.

The takeaway should map back to the desired outcome you wanted your audience to know, think, feel, or do when you defined their persona. There should be a connection between what you want for your audience and what they take away from the story. This helps make sure your story is meaningful for your audience.

How often have you sat through a presentation or story and wondered what it was about? I don't mean stories that are so rich that they leave you reflecting long after. I am referring to what happens in meetings every single day. Information is shared, but you're left scratching your head and wondering, *What am I supposed to do with this?*

These moments aren't your fault—the storyteller didn't stick the landing. Likely because they weren't even sure of the takeaway. That lack of clarity translated to your lack of understanding as the audience. The takeaway is the step most people skip in storytelling, but it's the very thing that can ensure your story resonates as intended.

The context, conflict, and outcome provide a high-level structure to the story. The takeaway provides the "so what" for the story—what you want the audience to experience. Even if you never say the takeaway aloud, just having it in mind helps you be more purposeful in the telling of the story.

Walt and Maria's stories have the same takeaway: it's critical for a leader to help each person feel seen and valued, regardless of their role. This made it easier to pair both into one story and connect them through an overall takeaway and desired outcome.

When you're planning your stories, start with this simple, memorable, four-part storytelling framework. Write out four sentences for the context, conflict, outcome, and takeaway to create structure and organize plot points, regardless of the order the story is told. This creates the structure for the rest of the story to be built upon. That is what we explore in the next chapter—how to meaningfully layer details onto your story.

SUMMARY

Outline Your Story Structure

See the checklists in the back of the book.

- Stories without a structure are hard to follow. The four-part story structure model gives you the flexibility to build out your idea for any setting.
- As you outline the story structure, don't worry about details or the order you will use to tell the story.
- Define the four-part story structure:
  - **Context:** What is the setting, who is involved, and why should we care?
  - **Conflict:** Where is the point where something happens? What is at stake? This is the fuel for your story.
  - **Outcome:** What is the result?
  - **Takeaway:** What is the idea that you want the audience to walk away with? How does this connect to the desired outcome for your persona?
- The four-part story structure is a tool you can use five minutes before a meeting to anchor the major points of a story or communication you're going to share. Using this structure makes it easier for the audience to follow and understand your story.

Manoush Zomorodi

Host of TED Radio Hour Podcast, *NPR*

How do you balance telling stories of other people and bringing your voice into the episode?

The role of the host is to be the proxy for the listener. I'm there to ask the question that just popped into your head. I am most successful when someone wonders, *Why isn't she asking . . . ?* and then I ask it. Once in a while, there is a question that only I would have. But I try to ask questions that anyone would have.

My job is to help the person I am interviewing tell their story better. Sometimes that means they need to relate to me a little more. Especially if they have been telling their story over and over again. Or they've been pitching investors. Or they're nervous. As a host, I ask myself, *How do I insert myself in a way that makes them as relaxed and as present in what they are going to tell me?*

How do you help someone tell their story better?

I don't just show up to an interview. Producers talk with guests and help them identify anecdotes they can share. "What was the day like? What were you wearing? How did you feel?" Some people can do that off the cuff. Other people need a few days to think through what they want to say. I try not to pre-interview people. I prefer to show up as more of a blank slate. But my producer has spoken to the person and filled me in.

In pre-production we consider, "What do we want to get out of this? What kind of talker are they? How can I support them?" Certain people you wind up and they go, and I barely have to say anything. Other people need me to be in conversation with them. And I love that too. I ask all the dumb questions. Which is the right thing to do when you are talking to a Nobel Prize winner who needs to be brought back to basics for the listener doing dishes.

The *TED Radio Hour Podcast* was already underway when you took over as host. How did you step into this role and make it your own?

You have a relationship with your storyteller, and you trust them. The first thing I needed to do was build trust with the audience so that they would keep coming back. To reassure them that the standard, quality, joy, and surprise they had been feeling would still be here. Then I used my particular flavor to go find new people to listen to the show.

Is there a lot done on the backend for editing of the episodes?

Our show is extremely highly produced. We love to use music and sound design to support a person's story. Sometimes I'm interviewing a scientist explaining a concept that doesn't have an exciting story. The producer and I work to edit their interview so that it is clear for the listener. Sometimes we decide to say, "Hold onto your seats, we're going to get really technical." Setting listener expectations is really crucial. If you don't, they get distracted and stop listening.

NINE

Adding Details That Matter

The first year I lived in New England, I learned of an anxiously awaited summer ritual: the opening of ice cream stands. Having grown up in Miami, I quickly recognized the importance of celebrating the survival of winter and anticipating the warm summer air on your neck and shoulders. After coordinating with friends, a date was circled on the calendar in red, and the countdown began. "You must be given proper initiation," I was told.

I didn't understand what that meant until I was standing in front of Kimball Farm in Westford, Massachusetts. Ten walk-up windows flanked the long farm building. After careful deliberation to choose the fastest line, we thoroughly studied the fifty flavors that hung on a white placard over each window. I breathed in the evening air mixed with the scent of vanilla and fresh waffle cones as my friends described how the dairy farm has been selling ice cream for over eighty years.

Overwhelmed with options, I couldn't decide between a cup or a cone. When I thought I had settled on a flavor, my eyes would follow someone walking away from a window with ice cream in hand. *Ooh, maybe I want that! What is it?* My excitement grew with each advancing step toward the ordering window.

The choice of flavor felt like one I had to get right, yet there was no wrong answer. *Am I in a fruity or a chocolate mood? Or do I want peppermint swirl?* I gave my order and handed over the money. A cup of mint cookie was pushed through the window with the spoon standing upright in the ice cream.

My lips turned up in a small, childlike smile as I lifted the spoon for the first cold and creamy bite. It was summer in a cup. I rhythmically raised the spoon as if in a trance, pausing only when brain freeze set in. Occasionally, I turned my head to lick ice cream dribbling down the side of the cup. As the spoon scraped the bottom, I stared off into the distance. My ice cream coma grew, and the initiation was complete.

I've had ice cream from my freezer far more times than I've ever gone out to get it. But I struggled to remember those at-home moments. I know they involved a bowl, a scoop, and a tub of ice cream. Occasionally some sprinkles or nuts. But I can't recall specific details. Getting ice cream outside your home is an event. It has vivid details, it imprints on your senses, and it's a mix of excitement and anticipation. It's memorable.

Communicating information to an audience is like getting ice cream from your freezer. It's fine and serves its purpose. But it often isn't memorable or engaging. Telling a great story is like going out for ice cream. It is so much more appealing, vivid, and memorable. And just like the variety of flavors, there are so many ways to tell a story based on the specific details you decide to include.

LAYER ON DETAILS AND EMOTIONS

The story structure provides the skeleton for your story to layer details and plot points upon and form the overall body.

Build out a story that provides context, relatable characters, and details. Leverage the third factory setting to connect the audience to what is already known or understood in their library of files. Help them feel like a member of the in-group or out-group as they experience the details of the story. Intentionally take the audience through moments of discomfort or joy.

As you layer the details of the story onto the skeleton, don't focus on the story order, senses, emotions, or how you will build tension just yet. First, expand the story to include the plot points and details.

I find it helpful to build out the story details in a few passes. The first time, I expand the structure to include the events and plot points of the story. The second time, I connect the audience to the setting and relatable characters. The third time, I add specific details. I often take a break between the second and third pass, letting the story (and me!) breathe. Coming back after a day or more makes it easier to see where additional detail is needed. Each pass acts as a constraint, helping you focus on the topic for that pass. This often generates more ideas than trying to create the story all at once. With practice, you may end up combining the second and third passes.

First Pass: What Are the Major Plot Points of the Story?

Expand the events of the story structure. Leverage the prompts in each section to help trigger your thinking and spark considerations. While you don't need to answer every question, you do want to create a few sentences describing the plot points for each of the four parts.

1. **The Context:** Who are the characters in the story? Why are they in the story? What do we need to know about them? What is the setting of the story? What details are familiar to your audience, even if they have never experienced the story firsthand? Include enough context so the audience cares and wants to hear more.

2. **The Conflict:** What is the moment of tension where something happens? What led to it? Who was involved? What happened? How does

this provide fuel for the story? What conflict do the characters experience? What needs to be resolved? Is this something your audience would identify with as an in-group or feel different as the out-group? Does the conflict feel uncomfortable?

3. **The Outcome:** What is the result of the conflict? What happens to the characters? How are they different than they were at the start of the story? What did they learn, gain, or lose? How did they grow? What is resolved?

4. **The Takeaway:** How does the story incorporate the theme of the takeaway? Are there pieces of the takeaway you want to include in the story?

Second Pass: All the Memorable Details

The second pass adds specific details to engage your audience in the story. Review your audience personas before doing this pass to include details familiar to them.

Time and Place

Include when and where the story takes place. This helps the audience immediately place themselves in the story. If I say, "Last year I was in Paris," your brain immediately pictures the Eiffel Tower. This helps you form a mental image of the story setting. Include enough details so the audience can form an image in their mind—even if they have never been there.

As I describe Maria walking into the elevator at work, you picture walking through a sunlit lobby to a bank of elevators. Without consciously willing it, you form a mental image of an office building.

When I introduce Walt heading into his last university exam, you visualize a campus. You may even picture a room where you took a class or exam. The time and place invite the audience to join the story, following along in their head with familiar events and places. The more details you give about the setting, the faster and easier the audience can visualize it. When and where is your story taking place?

Relatable Characters

Your audience's ability to connect with the story relies on the characters. They move the plot forward and provide conflict through their choices, desires, and actions.

Some people feel that stories should have a hero. I don't agree. Great stories often result from mistakes and failures. Characters need to be relatable, not heroes. We want to know why they do what they do, even if we don't like them or agree with their actions. To do that, we need to know some specific things about them.

What are the names of your major characters? It's not necessary to name every single person in the story. We need the names of people who play key roles in the story so we can keep track of them. Change names when you want to protect identities. I frequently use online baby name generators to protect my clients' identities.

Is it important for the audience to know the character's age or physical description? If it plays a role in your story or our understanding of the character, include it! I describe Maria's personality traits, but you don't know her current age, height, or physical description—or those of Ray, Walt, or Dottie. They weren't important to the story. Help the audience form a mental image by providing descriptions that are relevant to the plot.

What should the audience know about the personality of your characters? What mannerisms, attitudes, or beliefs are relevant to the story? Are they sarcastic and quick-witted? Do they speak with a Southern drawl? Does their phone perpetually show forty-seven unread messages? Do they interrupt others when they speak? Did they grow up in a city with three traffic lights? Give the audience specific details that leverage their assumptions and help form an understanding of the characters to make them relatable.

Maria knows your birthday, favorite food, and your last vacation because she likes people and wants them to feel seen. This prompts the audience to think of someone they know who pays attention and remembers little details. Ray smiles widely when he sees Maria approach the desk because most people barely nod at him. They're on a first-name basis. Each of these details makes the audience consider, *Would I brush past Ray each day?* Walt has straight A's and is expecting to ace the last exam of his university career, leveraging our assumption that he is smart, hardworking, and confident.

What conflict do the characters face? Is the conflict within themselves—needing to reconcile their behavior with their values? Is it a point of friction with someone else? Is it related to circumstances, actions, or desires? How does the conflict create tension throughout the story? How do the characters reconcile the conflict?

What are the emotions of the characters throughout the story? Do they feel dissatisfied or incomplete? Are they joyful or pulsing with excitement? Do their emotions change throughout the conflict? Don't *tell* us their emotions—*show* them. Describe their frustration by smacking their phone on the table. Show they are exhausted by having them pinch the bridge of their nose with their eyes closed. Draw us into their good mood by having their head nod with the beat of the background music. Invite the audience into the mind of the characters to experience what they feel.

We feel Walt's confusion when he turns over the exam paper and it's blank. We experience his shame as he realizes he doesn't know Dottie's name—something not in line with his values. He resolves the conflict by vowing to not make that mistake again. As the audience makes the same silent vow, they feel part of an in-group while moving through the uncomfortable moment. Bring the audience into the emotions of the characters and how they change throughout the story.

What Is at Stake?

A few years ago, I was traveling solo to the south of France for work. I landed at the Marseille Airport at 11:30 p.m. As I got my bag and went outside, the airport closed. My shoulders sagged when I realized there were no people or taxis around. The phone to call the taxis was broken, and I didn't have a phone number for the local taxi service. Even if I did, my French was not *magnifique*. I couldn't have communicated with them. I hadn't slept in twenty-three hours and was stranded and alone.

In a few sentences, we go from a trip to France to being trapped alone in a foreign airport overnight. The stakes are set, the tension is built, and your curiosity is piqued as you wonder how the story will unfold. As you build out the four-part story structure, describe what is at stake in the story or situation. These "What happened next?" moments will build and release tension throughout your story.

Third Pass: What Specific Details Can You Include?

Stories become memorable with specific details woven throughout the plot, events, and characters. These details help us visualize the story and give context to the characters, setting, and events. Capture attention and understanding with specific and descriptive details.

Are you eating ice cream, or are you eating a bowl of chocolate-chip ice cream with colored sprinkles and whipped cream? Is it a child, or is it a boy who loudly brags he is four and three-quarters? Is it a grocery list, or a grocery list with seventeen items? The specific details, like odd numbers, land differently. The more specific the details, the more vivid and memorable the story becomes for your audience.

The elevator doors keep closing on Maria. She knows your last vacation spot. Walt was a straight A student. These are all specific moments to help make the characters relatable, move the plot forward, and engage the audience.

There isn't a set number for the specific details you should include. Putting them in every sentence would bog down the story. Start by adding at least one specific detail in each section of the story. Err on the side of creating too many at this stage. As you review your story in later chapters, you will learn how to consider what doesn't move the story forward and can remove some.

Anchor to What Is Known

Anytime there is a major event covered in the news, a map of the location is shown. The nearest major city and landmarks are called out. When the Cathedral of Notre-Dame caught fire, news coverage included a map of Paris showing the location of the cathedral and the Eiffel Tower. The Eiffel Tower is a familiar landmark used to orient the audience and connect to what they know.

As you create your stories, consider details that anchor to what the audience knows and understands. These aren't limited to physical locations or landmarks. It may be a key date in time, like "three weeks before September 11, 2001 . . ." helping the audience picture what they understand for that time-frame. Physical items may also serve as an anchor. For many, a mobile phone is an important possession. Hearing that Maria's mobile phone fell down the elevator shaft connects the audience to what it would feel like to drop their phone.

Your anchor may be a comparison or metaphor. I once described the changes employees were experiencing in a company as if they were mid-air between two trapeze bars. The phrase "That's as annoying as a chirping smoke detector in need of batteries" simultaneously make you hear that chirp and experience the irritation. Hearing "The incision was the size of a paperclip," creates an immediate visualization of the length of the cut. "This idea is as refreshing as the cool side of the pillow" makes you immediately feel the cool sensation. These comparisons create understanding and help the audience become more engaged in the story. They remove the cognitive lift of the audience by automatically placing fully formed ideas into their heads.

Are There Unexpected Events in the Story?
As you build the plot of the story, include unexpected items to force your audience's brains to get out of lazy mode, spend calories, and slow down assumptions. Unexpected items can include plot points that unfold with twists. A character does something surprising. There is an unanticipated result. The audience makes an incorrect assumption. These don't have to be the most dramatic plot twists ever. These are those moments that make you say, "Huh, I didn't expect that" or "I didn't see that coming!"

You don't expect Maria to drop her phone down the elevator shaft—or that it will still work. You assume it's shattered, she won't get it back, or she will have to pay the expensive fee. Your brain says "What?" when Walt's final exam is one question. It's not surprising that he doesn't know Dottie's name, but it lands as a key plot point as we feel his shame. These unexpected events become opportunities to build tension. In future chapters we'll experiment on how to order your story to maximize this tension.

Unexpected items also include phrases or details. The actual plot point may not be unexpected, but a specific detail or phrase can make the brain take notice. Think of a favorite lyric in a song, line from a movie, or reaction you feel to a comedian saying an unexpected punchline. These phrases capture the audience's attention and often raise their eyebrows. They make the brain slow down and savor them, like a piece of rich Swiss chocolate. In my TED Talk I say, "Data doesn't change behavior—emotions do." It's quoted back to me frequently because it is unexpected, pithy, and captures attention. As you develop your stories, look for opportunities to include unexpected phrases.

These unexpected events make our brains engage with the story differently. As you take a second or third pass to expand the details of your story, consider what unexpected events, metaphors, phrases, and plot points you can include.

Eventually . . .

You may choose to write out your story, or you may prefer to outline it in bullet points and phrases. Experiment with what works best for you. I prefer initially scripting the story's details and flow. It helps me think through the story and be intentional about engaging the brain's factory settings. I can also catch areas where I have cheated the audience of details.

I recently wrote an article and laughed at a note from my editor. He had flagged my use of the word *eventually* in the piece and commented, "That is cheating your audience of detail." He was right! I hadn't even realized I had done that. *Eventually, someday, finally, at the end of the day, at last* . . . these are connecting words, but not descriptive ones. They cut corners and gloss over details. Better descriptions can replace them to create more meaning and engagement, and they often only require a few more words or maybe an extra sentence. This is why multiple passes help you catch places where you can give the audience more detail.

Details make the story structure come alive. They connect to what the audience understands, slow assumptions, and create vivid characters and imagery. Once the details are in place and characters are formed, we want to keep the audience's brain out of lazy mode. That is where we go next—how to help the audience experience the story through their senses.

---- **SUMMARY** ----

Adding Details That Matter

See the checklists in the back of the book.

- Layer on details and emotions to the four-part storytelling structure to form the overall body of the story.
- The details give the story context, relatable characters, and unexpected events to help anchor understanding for the audience.
- As you add details to your story, it's helpful to do so in a few passes. The first time, focus on the plot points and creating relatable characters. The second time, add in specific details and emotions.
- Set a time and place to engage the audience in the story.
- Give names to major characters. Include their ages, physical descriptions, or personality traits when important to the story.
- What conflict do characters have with themselves or others? What happens because of that conflict? What is at stake in the story?
- Specific details are memorable. Don't just tell us you're eating ice cream. Describe the specific flavor and any toppings.
- Anchor to what is known with landmarks, dates, metaphors, and examples to create additional ways for the audience to understand your story.
- Slow down assumptions by including unexpected events and phrases.
- Don't cheat the audience of details by using connecting phrases like "eventually." Describe what happened to get to that point.

Will Csaklos

*Screenwriter and Story Consultant; Former Senior Creative
Executive & Story Consultant, Pixar Animation Studios*

What is your "Story First" philosophy?

I worked at Pixar during, what I believe was, the second golden age of animation when the young studio produced a string of extraordinary hit movies: *Toy Story*, *Toy Story 2*, *Monsters, Inc.*, *Finding Nemo*, *The Incredibles*, *Wall-E*, and *Up*. My "Story First" philosophy was informed by working with some of the best storytellers in the world. Your movie can have the best actors, the most brilliant composers, the most original story artists, and stunning special effects, but if your story isn't sound from start to finish and through to its core, all of those fabulous elements combined will not turn an OK movie into a great movie.

What are common mistakes in scripts?

As a story consultant, I look for where scripts lag. Often, they have great openings but sag in the middle. Author Syd Field once said, "Put obstacles in front of your characters." A bridge goes out, or they blow a tire in a chase. Those things can give you a moment's bump but won't provide lasting story energy. The solution is to create sustainable rising action—the increase in conflict and complication—organically, based on character.

A lot of scripts miss two things. One: a constellation of characters that create conflict with others simply by how they go about attaining what they need and want in the world. Great scripts have a number of dynamic, conflictual relationships. When created correctly, each one becomes a story engine that helps infuse the narrative with dramatic power.

The second thing that will sink a script is the lack of verisimilitude—the semblance of truth. A reason to care about the characters and story. The first aspect of this is story logic—not in the sense of literary theory but in the sense of "does a jewel thief, finally released from prison, retrieve his hidden stash then leave it out on the dresser in his cheap hotel room before falling asleep?" Story logic asks the simple question, "Is this believable?" In the case of the jewel thief scenario, it is not. The moment that occurs, we disengage from the story.

The other essential aspect of verisimilitude in storytelling is emotional truth. Are the longings, fears, decisions, and actions of characters real, measured instantly by our knowing and by the depth of our experience as human beings?

I spoke at a conference after *Finding Nemo* was released. A young woman came up to me after. She told me she was from San Diego, had grown up with the ocean, and how much she loved *Finding Nemo*. "It was fantastic!" she blurted. "But real!"

Bingo!

We care about these characters and what becomes of them because of their emotional truth. In *Finding Nemo*, we never question Marlin's desire to protect his son. We understand Nemo's desire to get out on his own. Great storytellers make us care deeply, feel deeply, make us laugh and feel saddened to tears because of the truth of their portrayals. It's why we can be happily transported and transfixed by the plight of childhood toys and talking fish.

T E N

Make Us Feel Something

In June 1975, Steven Spielberg changed moviemaking with the premiere of *Jaws*. He made a generation nervous to swim in the ocean through masterful storytelling. Yet he struggled with how to tell this story, fearing it would stop his career before it could start.

When filming began, Spielberg had a script that centered around a shark. The mechanical sharks kept malfunctioning and sinking to the bottom of the ocean. As a joke, they were named Bruce after Spielberg's lawyer. They couldn't get through scenes without a malfunction. How do you make a movie about a shark without a shark?

For a brief moment of delusion, there was a debate about training a great white shark. But Spielberg decided to rewrite the movie, creating the sensation and illusion of the shark's presence. Cameras would take on the perspective of the shark. The audience didn't need to see the shark; they needed to feel its presence and let their brains fill in the rest.

Water splashes and music intensifies. Barrels move across the surface of the water. Swimmers are pushed in different directions. Boats suddenly lurch forward. You feel like the swimmers bobbing in the ocean as you watch the movie. Your brain tricks you into smelling the surf, tasting the saltwater, and even feeling the movement of the current. Your heart rate increases as you anticipate the presence of the shark. The movie is so vivid, most of us have thought of *Jaws* at least once during a day at the beach. And all of this was masterfully done through the illusion of a shark that engaged your senses.

The soundtrack is as big a character as the shark. Composer John Williams brilliantly put together those two alternating notes to build tension and get us to lean forward in our seats. The closer the attack, the faster the notes are played, without any space between them. In one scene, right when we expect the shark to attack, a kid pops up in the water with a fake fin strapped to his back. The tension is suddenly released and slowly built again, the music driving the pace. Great stories repeatedly build and release tension by piquing curiosity, raising the stakes and conflict, and then sharing something unexpected.

Constraints present the best ideas for storytelling. If Spielberg had a working mechanical shark, the movie wouldn't have been as gripping, and the shark wouldn't have been seen as realistic. Instead, he creatively leaned into senses and illusion to place you in the center of the story. The difference between a good story and a great story is how it engages the senses and emotions of the audience to make them feel and experience the same things as the characters.

| Constraints present the best ideas for storytelling. |

This stage of storytelling builds the body of the story, layering senses on top of the structure and details. Help the audience experience the events and details of the story. Make them see, hear, feel, taste, and smell what you describe.

I was giving a keynote for London Business School and asked for a person to help me demonstrate how to improve a story in under five minutes. Emma volunteered, and I asked her to think of a story to share about a vacation. She chose a bachelorette party she had attended a few years earlier that included a zip-lining adventure.

I first instructed Emma to tell the story without any prompting or coaching. She described receiving an invitation to a bachelorette weekend celebrating her friend getting married. When she learned zip-lining was one of the activities, she didn't want to go. Terrified of heights, she didn't want any part of that experience. Her friends convinced her to join the celebration, promising they would support her. When it was time to leave for zip-lining, she kept trying to tell herself that everything would be OK.

I then stepped in with her next round of instructions. "I want you to tell the same story again, but this time, focus on the colors, textures, smells, and the emotions in the story. What would we see, hear, feel, smell, or experience if we were there?"

Emma began her story again. "I stepped into the blue harness. My legs shook as it was tightened around my waist and legs. I clipped on the yellow helmet and started the long hike through the forest to the first zip-lining platform. I kept taking deep breaths of the sweet and damp pine scent. The trail was lined with evergreens, each a deeper shade of forest green. With each step forward, my boots grew heavier, and my fear increased. I could feel my heart beating in my ears. My friends were laughing and joking, but I could only focus on putting one boot in front of the other.

"As I climbed up on the launch platform, I wrapped one arm tightly around the tree. The dark brown bark made an imprint on my palm. Fear grew like a golf ball-sized lump in my throat as my turn approached. The instructors told me to let go of the tree and step forward. But instead, I turned toward the tree and wrapped my other arm around it, hugging it tightly and unable to let go. I could count the ridges of the bark as I faced the tree. My chest and my throat felt tight. I couldn't speak. The more my friends encouraged me to go, the tighter I hugged the tree."

In about three minutes, we took Emma's story from an interesting one to one where we are now hugging the tree with her. We experience her fear and dread, even if we aren't afraid of heights. It's easy to smell the sweet pine air and feel the heaviness of the boots. Whether we've zip-lined or not, we can understand and empathize with what she was feeling.

As you create your stories, intentionally do a pass focusing on making your audience feel something. Engage their senses and their brains.

DON'T TELL THE SENSES AND EMOTIONS—SHOW THEM

What are the colors in your story? How can you describe them? Don't just say, "The sunset was gold." Be vivid: "The sunset was like a glowing, flickering fire of orange, yellow, and gold." The more dynamic you are in your description, the easier it is for the audience to picture.

What do the characters feel, taste, smell, or hear? Show us, don't tell us. Place us in the story by having us feel the gusting wind turn our lips chapped and raw. Describe your friend's favorite cologne lingering on your clothes after hugging goodbye. Detail the calloused hands the character feels when greeting someone with a handshake. Don't just tell us it's raining. Let us hear the rain drumming against the window. Tell us how the laptop was unexpectedly lightweight—the same heft as the last paperback book you read. Help us feel the experience of walking into a room buzzing with energy and sensing everyone was talking about you moments before. Describe the stack of papers as thin as a mobile phone.

Your story may not include every sense. As you build it, consider the senses the major characters experience as they move through the story. Remember, the sense of smell is strongly linked to memory. Intentionally describing the smells in your story helps your audience easily place themselves in it through their memories with the scents.

Each sense not only helps engage the brain but also provides specific, memorable details for the audience to experience. You may think, *I can't describe colors or senses in business.* I disagree. We don't turn off our senses when we go to work.

Offices are full of smells: coffee brewing, inky printer cartridges, or a co-worker's leftover salmon being reheated in the break room. Conference rooms have sweaty pitchers of water, crumpled paper, brown trashcans, and the random paperclip on the floor. Retail environments have the hum of lights, cell phones dinging, the murmur of conversation, and the beeping of items being scanned. Teams spend hours debating whether the cyan or navy blue should be used in the chart for the presentation. Project risk is even assessed with red, yellow, and green status indicators, like a stoplight.

I'm not asking you to describe a field of flowers for your business presentation. You can engage the senses in a business context. "That is as clear as murky, grey water" or "We want employees to feel so inspired they run through walls." I once used the phrase "This process is as stale as a middle school locker room" to indicate when a change was needed. I also playfully told a manager, "I want to do that as much as I want to braid my eyelashes" when someone else volunteered me for a project. Not only did I get out of the project, but I was also handed an eye patch as a joke in the next meeting. Colors, senses, and emotions will help make your idea memorable for your audience, even in business settings. They are unexpected and make the brain pay attention.

Maria walks into the elevator, pushes the button, and her phone falls and bounces. Describing her actions stimulates the frontal lobe of your brain associated with movement. "Pushes the button" also activates the parietal lobe on the crown of your head, associated with touch. The *Whoosh!* sound I make to demonstrate the phone falling down the elevator shaft lights up the temporal lobes on the sides of your head, associated with hearing. In the first thirty seconds of the TED Talk, I intentionally engage your senses and emotions so that you experience discomfort.

What are your characters' emotions? Are they happy? Scared? Frustrated? Stressed? Delighted? Unsettled? Tired? How can you help the audience experience those emotions? Remember, don't tell us—show us what they look like. Instead of saying, "Emma has a fear of heights," tell us how Emma can't stop hugging the tree at the top of the zip line. Can you demonstrate your character is distracted by having him look at his phone every two minutes during a conversation? Is your character so shy she avoids looking others in the eye? Statements like, "He gave her the passcode to his phone" help your brain finish the thought by leveraging the assumption that he trusts her. Showing instead of telling stops the lazy brain and leverages assumptions to keep the listener engaged.

Bring the audience into the sweet nuances and vivid details of the story. "How do you know?" is a great question to ask yourself when reviewing your story. It will help you catch generalized statements like "Ricardo was cold" and change to "Ricardo couldn't stop shivering as his lips turned an indigo blue." This stimulates neural activity in the senses and lets us experience the same things as the characters. It's what makes us afraid of sharks in the ocean and grip our phones tighter when walking into elevators.

> Bring the audience into the sweet
> nuances and vivid details of the story.

As Maria tries to figure out what to do in the elevator threshold, the doors close on her repeatedly. You can almost feel the elevator doors bumping your shoulders as you read that. Walt's heart sinks when he realizes he doesn't know Dottie's name. He's embarrassed and mad at himself. We feel the same wave of shame when he realizes he doesn't know Dottie's name. His determination not to do that again reinforces our own. We are right next to him in the story.

What Makes This Story Messy or Complicated?

Zip-lining isn't complicated, but it is when you're afraid of heights. Dropping a phone down an elevator shaft is an inconvenience. Doing so with your badge, credit cards, and driver's license so you can't get into your office or car is messy. It becomes further complicated when you realize the cost, time, and effort it will take to replace each item. To get your audience to have empathy for your characters and your story, they need to relate to the situation. Not every story has to be messy or complicated. But when it is, even in a nuanced way, show it.

Connect your audience to the emotions that make the conflict messy or complicated. Why is the path forward challenging? What situation do your characters face where their choices aren't obvious or desirable? What feels heavy if the desired outcome isn't realized? Help the audience experience the messy and complicated elements of the story.

Maria is facing paying a lot of money to get her phone back or the inconvenience of replacing her phone and several critical items. Walt feels embarrassment and shame for not knowing Dottie's name—something that is important to him. He is forced to reconcile his own questioning of leadership values.

Seeing What You Can't Unsee

In business presentations, you often hear a reference to "The Money Slide." This is the one slide in a presentation that clarifies the point of the presentation and the takeaway. It's often the "decision-making" slide that brings things to a culmination and lands the strongest takeaway. I've always thought of it as the slide where people see the things that they can no longer unsee. A great story is your money slide. It's going to build an idea and awareness that the audience can no longer look past and unsee.

Charities are masters of helping people see what they can't unsee. They describe the problem by telling a story that connects you to senses, emotions, and challenges. They often tell stories to intentionally make you feel different and a member of the out-group. Through those stories, you see things you can no longer unsee.

Charity: Water helps people understand the challenge of not having access to clean water by telling stories of individuals, like Jean. He is a child who carries a five-gallon can to a pond to fetch water for his family. He makes this walk five times a day, carrying the bucket on his head, his bare feet avoiding pebbles and rocks on the dirt path.

This pond is full of cloudy, stagnant water that you would never drink. Yet it is the only water available to his family. Without it, they don't have water for cooking, bathing, or planting. When he is sick, his family struggles to make their water stretch. He is unable to go to school because his family relies on him for the water. They are stuck in a perpetual loop, unable to change their circumstances in life.

You now understand the problem of not having access to clean water differently. You imagine the weight of the bucket on your head and the feel of the dirt path with pebbles under your feet. It's easy to recognize the impact on this family and others all over the world. The story expands to explain that one in ten people globally don't have access to clean water. Before the story, it's easy to hear that statistic but not connect with it. It takes on new meaning after hearing Jean's story. A great story can introduce an idea so the audience views it differently.

As you build your stories, what do you want people to see that they can't unsee? How do you take an idea and help your audience connect with it, so they think and act differently? The stories of Walt and Maria don't necessarily introduce ideas that people don't already know. But they may not be practicing them as regularly as they would like. Walt wasn't, which is why he vowed to always know the Dotties in his life. You can't help but wonder if you would have known her name. You may have even made the same vow to introduce yourself to someone in your life after connecting with the story and idea.

Details, senses, and emotions are layered on the story structure to create a dynamic, memorable story for the audience. Their placement in the story directly impacts the experience of it. That is further amplified through the order in which the story is told, which can either build and release tension or make a story fall flat. That is where we go in the next chapter—experimenting with the right sequencing for your stories.

SUMMARY

Make Us Feel Something

See the checklists in the back of the book.

- Descriptions that engage the senses increase neural activity, keep your brain out of lazy mode, and immerse the audience in the story.
- Don't tell the senses. Show them so the audience sees, hears, feels, tastes, and smells the same thing as the characters.
- The sense of smell is closely related to memory. Engage it in your stories so the audience connects their related memories and experiences to the topic.
- Connect the audience to what is messy or complicated. Describe emotions and senses of the characters so they understand what is at stake. This not only builds tension, but also helps the audience think of similar moments they have experienced.
- Show the emotions of the characters without telling us. Don't tell us the character is frustrated. Describe how they cut someone off in conversation, refusing to have the same conversation again.
- Help your audience see what they can't unsee. Take an idea and connect the audience with it so they think and act differently.

Colby Webb

Executive Global Business Leader, former Chief Marketing Officer

You tell stories for a living. What is the most important story you've ever told?

Marketing is in an age of "story doing" and not just "storytelling." People want to know what you stand for or how you will make their life better. I didn't realize the most important story I would ever tell wasn't one that I invented, but one that would reinvent me.

I have always been an animal lover and advocate. Despite regularly donating, volunteering, and fostering, I had not yet come to understand the larger issue behind the animal welfare system and the challenges that many breeds face—especially pit bulls.

Then, twelve years ago, I was volunteering at an event and saw a flyer with the photo of a two-year-old pit bull named Dan. I immediately knew I was meant to be his best friend. I adopted him, and he changed my life forever. Dan opened up an entirely new world to me— one of both fulfilling opportunities and horrific realities. I learned that pit bull-type dogs make up most of the dogs in New York and national animal shelters, largely because of a dog fighting past that continues to haunt them. They are overbred, misunderstood, and vilified—preventing them from finding social acceptance or homes willing to adopt them.

In recent years, only one in six hundred pit bulls was adopted nationwide. Seventy-five percent of shelters euthanized all pit bulls regardless of their behavior, age, or physical health. Their only flaw was the label "pit bull" or "pit bull mix." This isn't even a real breed category. It's a catch-all term for a dog with a square head and almond-shaped eyes. The overwhelming majority are gentle, loyal, and loving, but stigmatized due to irresponsible owners, misinformed media coverage, and illegal dog fighting.

When I met Dan, many municipal shelters used the same intake as prisons with a photo, behavioral assessment, and quarantine. The dogs looked terrified and unfriendly in the photos. Between the bad photo and "pit bull" label, the odds of adoption were slim.

It occurred to me that they didn't just need more people willing to adopt. There was a story here that needed to be re-told. A new set of actions needed to be taken, and the pit bulls needed "rebranding" to showcase their true nature and help change their fate.

I started the Sav-a-Bull charity to educate and aid in the rescue, training, and adoption of pit bulls into loving and capable homes. The animals were featured as positive family and community members in the news, films, and books.

The Sav-a-Bull charity partnered to create the "Boroughbred" campaign for the Animal Care Centers of New York. We worked with professional photographers and creative teams that donated their time to describe New York as a resilient melting pot of people and animals. New York's pets are a special breed. None should be vilified.

Billboards and sides of buses were covered with stories and images highlighting the affectionate and playful nature of pit bulls. Their contagious smiles and regal stature made people reconsider the breed. They weren't ferocious; they were future friends. Dan even appeared on a video Times Square billboard giving kisses to every person walking by. During the campaign, every single dog was adopted. This campaign is still active online.

Ever since the day I adopted Dan, he'd put his head in my lap and look up at me with his beautiful golden eyes as if to say, "Thank you," but I am the grateful one. Dan made me a better person and gave me purpose. All the good things I've accomplished are a result of the day I adopted him. The day I promised to tell his story, and the story of others like him, to help people feel what I do for these incredible dogs.

This story isn't over. Sav-a-Bull is beginning animal education with younger people using Dan's story. No human or animal should have the stigma of a label deciding their fate. Stories can change the conversation, can save lives, and can demonstrate all dogs deserve to be treated with love and compassion.

ELEVEN

Sequence Your Story

One of my favorite movies is *Good Will Hunting*. I love this movie for many reasons. It's a unique story with complicated characters. Matt Damon and Ben Affleck wrote this movie because they were struggling to get cast in roles. The soundtrack featuring Elliott Smith is somber and hauntingly beautiful. And it has a scene that is the perfect example of how to tell a non-linear story.

The main character is Will Hunting, played by Matt Damon. Will is a genius who has been abused and bounced around foster care and juvenile detention. With a lifetime of people betraying him, Will struggles with trust and maintaining relationships. He works as a janitor at MIT as part of his parole. A professor catches him solving a ridiculously hard math equation, recognizes his genius, and decides to mentor him. There is one condition: Will has to work with a therapist on his past trauma. Enter Robin Williams as Dr. Sean Maguire, a widowed therapist who grew up in South Boston as Will did.

About halfway through the movie, there is a scene with a counseling session in Sean's office. Will asks Sean, "Do you ever wonder what your life would be like if you never met your wife?"

This introduces the theme and takeaway of what will be explored in the scene: Would your life be different if you didn't meet and marry your wife?

Sean acknowledges it as an important question. He admits that relationships have bad times but that they make you aware of the good moments. Will asks if he regrets meeting his late wife. Sean says he doesn't regret a single day with her.

The audience now knows the outcome of the story: even though his wife died, Sean doesn't regret meeting her, even with the hard times they experienced. Knowing the outcome and how it supports the takeaway isn't enough. We haven't connected with why Sean believes this. We don't know what took place to help form this belief.

Will asks, "When did you know she was the one?"

This introduces the conflict in this story. We are at a moment of tension and about to go on the journey with Sean. He will take us back to the beginning and give us the context for the story. Then he will move forward until he returns to the conflict. As the audience, we don't even realize that will happen. We just want to know how Sean knew he was meant to be with his wife.

Sean responds with "October 21, 1975."

This is a wonderfully unexpected and specific detail. Your interest is piqued along with Will's. It releases tension because it is specific, and it builds it because you need more context. Why this date—what was going on that day? Sean describes the day as game six of the World Series. He slept outside with friends to get tickets. Even if you aren't a fan of baseball or the Boston Red Sox, you understand this day is a big deal and important to Sean. This is reinforced by Will's shocked reply: "You got tickets?!"

At this point, the context is set. We know when the story takes place, who is involved, and we have a reason to care. Tension is built as we want to know what happened. Sean releases the tension just a smidge. He describes hanging out with his friends at a local bar pregaming before they went into the stadium. "And in walks this girl." A statement said in passing. A seed that is to sprout after we forgot it was planted.

Sean shifts and describes the game that went into extra innings. In the twelfth inning, Red Sox player Carlton Fisk was up to bat. He clocks the ball down the left-field line. Everyone in the stadium is yelling at the ball to stay fair. Carlton Fisk gestures wildly over his head as if that will make the ball land inbounds. Luck is on his side. The ball hits the foul pole and bounces fair. The Red Sox score and guarantee a game seven.

Sean and Will get up and run around his office chairs as though they are the players running bases. They act out the story in real-time as Sean describes the excitement of the day. We can hear the crowd cheering and almost smell popcorn in the air. Will matches Sean's excitement and yells "I can't believe you had tickets to the game! Did you rush the field?"

We are at peak tension in this story. Sean masterfully releases it. His energy, pitch, and pace drop several levels as he goes back to the seed he planted at the top of the story.

"No, I wasn't at the game. I was in the bar having a drink with my future wife."

Boom. We are back to where we started. At the conflict.

It's unexpected. It's specific. It almost makes your brain hit a speed bump and go, *"Huh?"* because you're expecting him to describe rushing the field or celebrating with his friend. You don't expect him to say he never went to the game. Will's brain hits that speed bump alongside the audience as he exclaims incredulously, "Who are these friends of yours that could let you get away with that!? What did you say to them?"

Sean replies: "I slid my ticket across the table to them and said, 'Sorry, guys, I've got to go see about a girl.'" He describes his future wife as a stunner, and his friends could see in his eyes that he meant it. They took his ticket and left while he had a drink with the woman who would become his wife. He never regretted talking to her, getting married, or taking care of her when she became sick.

With that, the story has come full circle. We've gone on a journey with Sean. We know he met his wife in a bar on the same day as game six of the World Series (the context). That he gave his ticket to his friends to have a drink with his future wife instead of going to the game (the conflict). He never regrets meeting his wife or their life together (the outcome). And as a result, he doesn't wonder if his life would be different or wish he hadn't met her (the takeaway).

The scene works so well because of the sequencing. Getting the takeaway and outcome upfront creates curiosity. You know what happens in the end, but you don't know why or how that happens. The specific details make you intrigued. The story takes you on an arc, using unexpected sentences, tension, and plot points to hold your attention.

The scene could have started with Will asking, "How did you meet your wife?" Sean could've sequentially taken us through their meeting, their wedding, her death, and his lack of regrets. But it's too predictable. Flipping the order allows the story to be revealed with unexpected elements. This does two things. It grabs our attention, so we want to know more. And it creates a stronger understanding and meaning for the takeaway of the story.

SEQUENCING STORIES

Great stories use sequencing and unexpected plot points to reveal the story in the most compelling way. The sequencing is what helps immerse the audience and to build and release tension.

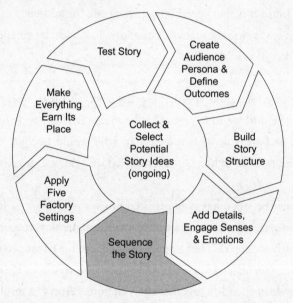

You've gathered and prepared ingredients for a story through the previous steps. Sequencing helps you look through them and determine which recipe you will make. The way you sequence a story has a big impact on the arc and audience experience.

Plot versus Character

As a child, you listened to fairy tales that often began with "Once upon a time" and then unfolded the beginning, middle, and end, concluding with "and they lived happily ever after." It is a sequential and predictable unfolding of a plot meant to entertain. The story arc typically features the path of the plot or the characters.

Character-driven stories focus on the people in the story—their thoughts and conflict. The characters undergo an arc, ending the story with new growth and realizations. They experience some change by the end. Plot-driven stories focus on external events and results. Characters play key roles in plot-driven stories, but the focus is on the events of the story and less on the transformation of the characters.

Would your audience be more impacted by the changes the characters undergo or by the events of the story? Is it a combination of both? Consider which way your story tilts. Plot-driven stories often lean into descriptions of what you see, hear, feel, taste, or smell in the story during the events. Character-driven stories connect you to the emotions of the character and how they shift and evolve over the story. Both versions engage the senses and emotions. But there is a slightly different tilt to each as the details unfold.

Maria's story is plot driven. We experience what happens to her and the result of her actions. We connect with her frustration and intentional engagement with people. But Maria doesn't go through a personal arc in the story. Walt's story is character driven. We first meet him as a CEO, then go back in time to learn about an event that contributed to his leadership values today. After failing the exam and feeling personal shame, he vows to be different. We feel the shift he makes as he vows to always know the Dotties in his life.

Perspective

From which perspective is your story best told? Is it one of the main characters or your point of view? Consider how the story may shift based on the perspective it is told from. If Maria's story was told from her perspective, the story might have slightly different takeaways. We'd learn more about her mindset when intentionally connecting with people. She would describe what she appreciates about Ray. We'd experience her surprise and delight as she learns about the impact she's had on Ray. Experiment with different perspectives to explore which best helps you build the outcome for your audience.

Determining the Story Order

There are many ways to sequence a story. Experiment to find the one that feels best for each story. Write major plot points from the context, conflict, outcome, and takeaway on different Post-its. Move them in different orders. Notice which feels the most compelling for your audience without feeling too predictable.

Linear Stories

A linear story is told in the order of beginning, middle, and end. These are chronological and describe events in the order they unfold. Linear stories work well when there is a complicated timeline or events that are hard to track. Unexpected elements tend to come toward the end of these stories. These create an arc by building to the conflict and releasing it with the outcome and end of the story.

Stories with Flashbacks

Sitcoms and movies often use this technique to pause a linear story to flashback in time and reveal a specific piece of information. The flashbacks give context to characters, provide insights into the conflict faced, or set up information that will impact the story.

Flashbacks are often told in the linear format of beginning, middle, and end. But somewhere in the beginning or middle, the story pauses to share a flashback. Then it resumes the story where it paused. Tension is built through what is revealed in the flashback itself. The interruption of the story slows assumptions, making the audience raise an eyebrow and wonder what they will learn. These flashbacks help the audience quickly learn character or plot information integral to the story.

Circular

These stories end where they begin. Often starting at the conflict, they move forward to the end and loop back to the beginning before working their way back to the conflict. The scene from *Good Will Hunting* is an example of a circular story. These work well when you drop the audience in at the point of conflict. The outcome is known. Tension is built because context is lacking.

Circular stories don't dip their toe in the water and slowly wade in. They back up and take a running leap to jump into the conflict of the story. It's unexpected, sets the stakes, and engages the brain.

Begin with the End

Like circular stories, these start with the end of the story and the outcome. From here, they can either work backward to the conflict and then the beginning. Or they can go to the beginning and build on the conflict. Even if the end is revealed, the lack of context for the outcome builds tension. As these stories conclude, they often revisit the end with new plot points and insights from characters.

These are the "You might wonder how I got here . . ." stories often used to begin movies or social media posts. Comedians often use this flow. They introduce the end of the story—often a personal experience. Then they take you through the arc of the story. Even though you know the outcome, you're glued to the story with the unexpected details woven throughout. This format works when you have unexpected details about the characters or plot that are more compelling than the outcome.

Parallel Story

These include multiple storylines that share something in common—people, plot points, or a theme. You tell them both under the arc of an overall story. I will often use parallel stories when I am trying to build a new idea or challenge an idea the audience holds. By combining multiple stories, you naturally encourage the audience to compare ideas and gain a different perspective.

The opening story of the TED Talk is a parallel story. Both Walt and Maria's stories are connected by the theme of helping people feel seen and valued. The combination creates an overarching story resulting in a more impactful takeaway for the audience.

Parallel stories work great when you want to take your audience out of their day-to-day context to connect to an idea or emotion. The combination of stories slows down the ability for assumptions and can help build new thinking.

Changing Perspectives

Sometimes it is helpful to tell a story from multiple perspectives. These end up being a few stories combined within one. A story could be told from one perspective and then picked up from a different perspective. Flashbacks may be included to give context from a different perspective. Two different perspectives could contrast specific plot points of the story. Documentaries often use this approach. Different perspectives are shared about the subject and woven into an overall story.

Changing the voice in a story can be tricky, especially when it's in writing. If you decide to include multiple perspectives, make sure your audience understands when new voices come in and who they are. You also want to make sure the different perspectives don't provide repetitive information. This will make the reader lose interest. This format works well when there are different perspectives the audience isn't considering around your desired outcome.

The story about Walt and Maria is told from one perspective: mine. While it is a story about other people, my perspective is consistent. Consider if you need different perspectives in your story or if you're telling the story from your perspective.

Compare, Contrast, "Imagine If..."

If you have ever participated in a visioning or strategy session, you were likely asked to visualize, "Imagine it is two years from today . . ." These stories connect an audience to a mindset or idea. They compare what is known and understood with future possibilities.

I was working with the head of communications in a Fortune 500 engineering company. He wanted his team members to partner with each member of the C-suite team to develop messaging. Together, we wrote an "Imagine if . . ." story that was a press release for a year out, detailing the team's success. It even included quotes for what they wanted the C-suite to say about their work. This connected the team to the aspiration of where they wanted to be in a year and identify the shifts necessary to achieve their goals.

These stories are helpful when you're trying to help your audience embrace change, notice progression, or connect to something aspirational.

STARTING YOUR STORY

Have you ever opened the first page of a book and found the first line intrigued you to keep reading? An opening hook grabs your attention, sparks intrigue, and makes you curious to hear more.

Do the same thing in your own story, regardless of how it is sequenced. The opening of the story will either capture the audience's attention or make them lose interest. Grab the audience's attention so they have a compelling reason to continue with the story.

Start with a Question

Questions are great pattern interruptions for our brain. A question nudges the brain by asking, "What do you think?" The audience is invited to participate. The question needs to spark curiosity and be intriguing enough to make the brain spend some calories.

Start with a Statement About the Theme of the Story

One of my favorite TED Talks is "The Museum of Four in the Morning," given by the performance artist Rives. He starts with this sentence: "The most romantic thing to ever happen to me online started out the way most things do—without me, and not online." He plants a seed for what is to come and sets off on a story that returns to that statement at the very end. With this sentence, he creates intrigue, sets the context, and makes you want to learn more about this romantic experience.

Use the Unexpected

I begin this book with "I have one brown eye and one green eye." While this trait isn't rare, it's uncommon and unexpected. Unexpected openings capture attention. Take a regular opening to your story and challenge yourself to make it unexpected. Sometimes I challenge myself to come up with five or ten different opening sentences to spark creativity. Many of them won't work, but my best ideas often aren't the first few. They emerge after challenging myself to keep thinking.

Appeal to Curiosity

As soon as you learned Maria's phone fell down the elevator shaft, you likely thought, *What happened!?!* One sentence in, and you want to know what happens next. Remember when you mapped the story structure and had to answer the context question: "Why should your audience care?" That helps identify what is interesting about your story. How can you bring that into the opening to spark curiosity?

It may take a few different tries to sequence your story and create your opening. Experiment to feel what is compelling for your audience. Give your story space. Take note of what you want to do next, and then walk away. Remember, our brain hates for things to be incomplete, and it will continue working on it in the background. The next time you come back to it, you will have the benefit of new insights and a fresh perspective. The right sequence often reveals itself with space.

Up to this point, we've been creating the story with events, characters, details, senses, and emotions. Editing is the next step in the story creation process. The next chapter introduces how to validate that you've leveraged the Five Factory Settings to engage the brain and ensure everything earns its place in the story.

SUMMARY

Sequence Your Story

See the checklists in the back of the book.

- Does your story focus on the growth and evolution of the characters? Does it lean toward the plot of the story? Or both?
- Choose the best flow for your story. Put major plot points on Post-its, and experiment moving them in different order to find the best sequencing.
  - **Linear:** beginning, middle, and end.
  - **Flashbacks:** linear stories that pause and share a flashback that sets context before continuing.
  - **Circular:** often starting with conflict, these start and end at the same place.
  - **Begin with the end:** beginning with a known outcome, the journey to it is revealed throughout the story.
  - **Parallel story:** multiple stories that share people, plots, or themes in common.
  - **Change perspective:** stories told from the perspective of different characters.
  - **Compare, Contrast, "Imagine If . . .":** visioning or strategy sessions.
- Determine the perspective the story is most compellingly told from.
- The start of the story should capture attention whether with a hook, a question, a statement or by appealing to the curiosity of the audience.

Evan Skolnick
Video Game Writer and Narrative Designer

How do you write stories for video games?

A video game is one of the most complex and challenging forms in which to develop stories. The process is very iterative, dynamic, and collaborative. It's not like a movie, where the writer hands off their script to a team so they can bring the story to the screen. The narrative design is a core part of development that happens in collaboration with the entire team, including designers, animators, and programmers.

Unlike storytelling for film or television, the narrative isn't leading the charge in game development. Players generally come to games for the gameplay first, not the story. Your role as a game writer is to enhance gameplay, not step on it. Narrative can make a good game great, but it can't make a bad game good.

The narrative should be intertwined with the gameplay as much as possible. One of the first questions I ask when consulting on a new project is, "Who is the player, and what can they do?" Because the story should be built around those details.

How does choice factor in the stories for video games?

An important aspect of game storytelling is the concept of player agency. We want to give players the feeling of as much control as possible, or at least the illusion of choice. Even with a linear design, there's often not just one perfect outcome. But supporting choices and branching can be very challenging, and often creates tracking complications for designers. For one game, I had this giant spreadsheet posted on the wall keeping track of all the characters and their arcs. My main fear was that a non-player character might die and then pop up in a scene or level somewhere else!

It's also important to understand that players have different interest levels in the story. When I was working as lead writer on *Marvel: Ultimate Alliance 2*, we categorized players into three different types: skippers, dabblers, and explorers. Skippers don't care about the story and skip cutscenes. Explorers are obsessed with the story, and they read every little lore item and listen to every audio log they can find. Dabblers are everyone in the middle. You have to make the story work for each type of player.

There are also dynamic elements you don't encounter in other media. For example, if you're playing a military combat game, you may hear another character yell, "I'm hit!" We need different versions of that line because they may get hit fifteen different times. A character saying the exact same thing twice in a row takes you out of the experience entirely. This can require tens of thousands of systemic dialogue lines to be written, recorded, and set up to trigger appropriately. It can get overwhelming!

When done right, game stories are built in support of gameplay and the player's desire. The narrative runs through everything, providing context for gameplay scenarios and helping the game make sense, without getting in the player's way.

TWELVE

Make Everything Count

Damien Chazelle is a film director, producer, and screenwriter. He's directed Academy Award-winning movies like *Whiplash* and *La La Land*. While editing *La La Land*, he felt some of the musical numbers slowed the storyline. One was the opening scene—a colorful dance number on an overpass in Los Angeles ending with the introduction of the two main characters.

Damien's solution was to take every musical number out of the movie. For a year, he edited the storyline and experimented with pacing. He focused on creating an arc for the audience to connect with the characters' emotional growth. Each musical number had to earn its way back into the movie by meeting specific criteria. *Does this advance the story forward? If cut, would anything be lost?*

Editing is as important as creating the story. It's a combination of adding, cutting, and testing. Through editing, the real story emerges. There are two parts to editing your story. The first part ensures you have leveraged the Five Factory Settings of the Brain. The second part involves making everything earn its place.

APPLY THE FIVE FACTORY SETTINGS OF THE BRAIN

Now that your story is built, it's time to make sure you've effectively engaged the brain and leveraged the Five Factory Settings. Begin refining the story only after you've had a break from creating it. Whether an hour, day, or week, the pause between creating and editing the story will give you space to see your story more clearly.

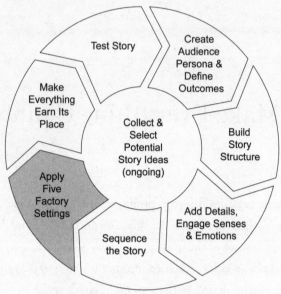

Lazy Brain, Assumptions, Library of Files

As a reminder, the first three Factory Settings of the Brain are that our brain is lazy, makes assumptions, and categorizes information into a library of files of knowledge and experiences that inform the brain's predictions. In storytelling, these three are often engaged in combination. Details you might include to nudge the brain out of lazy mode may also slow down assumptions or connect to what is understood in the library of files. Review the following items to validate that you have effectively engaged the brain in your story. These are also included in the checklists at the end of the book.

Build and Release Tension

There should be an arc to your story—where it builds and releases tension at least once and possibly multiple times throughout. This forces the brain to focus and slows down assumptions.

There are different ways to make sure your story builds tension. Incorporate unexpected details or events in the plot. Escalate events toward the conflict.

Help the audience feel the increasing stakes in the story. Use time or deadlines as a constraint. Describe characters' struggles—with themselves or each other. Use a clever phrase or humor to release tension. Add in an unexpected detail. Sequence the story so it doesn't feel predictable.

As you review your story, look for opportunities to swap the obvious and predictable with the unexpected. Can you shift when key points are revealed? Is there a different sequence or perspective that adds to the tension? Do your characters say or do something surprising? Can you expand the characters' struggles? Identify one thing you can do to increase the tension in your story.

Relatable Characters

How easily does the audience relate to your characters—even if they don't like them? Can your audience understand their situations, choices, and consequences, even if they wouldn't make the same decisions? Why do the characters do what they do? What are their emotions? How do they grow and change through the story? Where do they struggle or get stuck? What are their relevant physical or personality traits? Can you anchor the characters' behaviors, descriptions, mindset, or emotions to something already understood by the persona you created for your audience? What is one thing you can add to make the major characters relatable?

Engage the Senses

What does the audience see, hear, feel, smell, or taste through the experience of the story? Where can you engage the senses to trigger what is known and familiar? Is her voice so soft that everyone in the room must lean forward to hear her? Does the stress of the situation feel like carrying thirteen books in a backpack? Does the conference room smell like stale popcorn?

What dynamic colors are in the story beyond the standard red, blue, green, and yellow? Is the blue a deep turquoise you might find in the surrounding water of a Caribbean Island? Was the phone case a sunflower yellow?

What emotions do the characters experience? How do we know they are sad, mad, frustrated, exhausted, or joyful through their mannerisms and expressions? Are they so exhausted that they fell asleep on the couch in work clothes? Are they so frustrated they walked away for a few minutes? What is one thing you can add to the story to make us dynamically experience the story as if we were in it?

Details

In each major section of the story, have you incorporated at least one specific detail? Where can you turn pie into pumpkin pie, or describe the echo of heels clicking across the floor of the lobby? Has the supply chain collapsed like an imploded building? Was the client meeting as tense as driving when your car's gas gauge is on empty? Did the product feel weightless, like a cotton ball? Was the character from a town that was so small that there were a hundred people in his high school class? Where can you incorporate a specific, memorable detail or metaphor and connect to the audience's understanding?

Cut the Common

Each time you use common phrases or expressions like *throw the baby out with the bathwater, at the end of the day, stick out like a sore thumb, felt like an odd duck,* or *to be honest,* you are giving your audience's brain permission to stop listening. These overused phrases cut corners in communicating and hand the brain a pillow to slide into lazy mode. What common phrases and expressions are in your story? How can you replace them or remove them altogether?

Share Your Specific Perspective

How have you made the story personal and one that only you can tell? Does the audience know why you are sharing this story? How is your perspective different from someone else's? What is your fingerprint on this story? What is important to you about the story? What insights have you gained? What excites you about the story? Your perspective is unique. Don't narrate it with "I am telling this story because . . ." Show us why you're telling this story.

In- and Out-Groups, Seek Pleasure, Avoid Pain

The last two Factory Settings often work in combination as well. In- and out-groups help you feel a sense of belonging or differences. Neurochemicals reinforce experiences that create comfort or pleasure, or help you get out of uncomfortable settings. Consider how you have intentionally leveraged these in the audience's experience of the story.

In- and Out-Groups

How does your story help the audience think, *Yep, I've been there*, or, *Whoa— that is so different from my life and experiences*? Do you want your audience to feel a sense of belonging with the characters in the story? Or do you want them to notice their differences? Have you included emotions that allow them to identify with the plot and characters of the story? Is your intent to connect them to what they want to become or gain? How might they recognize the similarities or differences in their circumstances, thoughts, and experiences from the story? If you told the story from a different perspective, does it change the experience for the audience? What is one thing you could add to help your audience feel a sense of belonging with the story—or intentionally feel different?

Familiar or Uncomfortable

Do you want the audience to experience an uncomfortable or heightened moment—like learning about dropping a phone down an elevator shaft? Or discomfort—like hearing about someone losing all their personal data because of infected and corrupted computer files?

Do you want your audience to feel comfort or familiarity—like stories about employees receiving an award for identifying and solving a problem? Are you able to connect the audience to the higher aspiration of something through your story? Like the person who isn't buying a car but is buying a lifestyle. Does your story make the audience vow not to do something? Like not allow any vacation time to expire after hearing about an employee who lost two weeks of unused vacation. What is one thing you can do to intentionally help connect your audience toward feeling familiarity or discomfort in your story?

MAKE EVERYTHING EARN ITS PLACE

In a great story, everything has earned its place. Each item should move the story forward, reveal something about characters, or intentionally engage the Five Factory Settings of the Brain. Stories aren't complete until they have been trimmed. There are different approaches to tightening stories. Some people automatically cut 10 percent of the content once drafted. Others work through the piece and tighten what sticks out as odd. On my first drafts, I write freely. Then I challenge myself to cut to a specific word count. I end with a final pass to make sure everything earns its place.

Go line-by-line through your story and ask yourself: *Does this earn its place? Does this advance the story? If this were cut, would anything be lost? Does this create confusion and need something added or removed?*

If the item can be removed and it doesn't impact the plot, specific details, or emotions, take it out. Notice what feels different. What is important to you as the storyteller often isn't as important to your audience. Don't strip your story of all the details and senses that engage the brain. But when something slows the pacing of the story, try removing it.

Back in the Elevator . . .

I don't tell the end of the elevator story in the TED Talk. It's implied that Maria gets her phone back, but you don't know for sure. We don't know what she says to Ray in response to his help. It isn't necessary for the takeaway. It worked better to switch to Walt's story, which concludes with his vow in the exam room.

More could have been added to both stories, but they wouldn't have added to the takeaway. I connect you to Maria's frustration and Walt's shame. Each sentence advances the story forward to engage your senses and reinforce the outcome that having people feel seen and valued is critical as a leader.

DO I HAVE TO DO ALL OF THIS?

"I just want to tell a story. Do I need to go through all these steps?"

Each step ensures you're effectively engaging the audience's brain and working toward your desired outcome. The methodology helps you figure out the message you want to communicate with clarity. Meaningful layers are then added for deeper engagement. The first few times you follow the process, it may feel slow. You're internalizing a new skill and forming new neural pathways. It's the same as learning a new sport. You don't perform perfectly on the first day. Practice the components, and your abilities strengthen.

Storytelling is a compounding skill. The more you do it, the faster and easier it becomes. You will figure out how you best find your ideas and create stories. The ability to see the best flow for each story will become innate. Intuition will form around the specific details to include and senses to engage. The more you do it, the faster you move through the process while combining steps. If you want storytelling to be something you do with ease, just start.

"I want to tell a story in real-time. I can't do all this."

The more you practice developing and telling stories, the easier it becomes to do in real-time. Focus on three things when telling a story in real-time:

1. Before any potential interaction, think about your audience and what you want them to know, think, do, or feel. This is a good habit, regardless of whether you plan to tell a story. The answers help you plan for the interaction and shape any communication toward that outcome.
2. Tell the story through the four-part story structure. Describe the context, conflict, outcome, and takeaway to prevent a meandering story.
3. Add in at least one specific detail in your story and engage one sense.

Each person's storytelling style is different. Experiment with telling both prepared and real-time stories. Tell off-the-cuff stories in meetings and conversations. Practice prepared stories for presentations. Figure out which steps feel natural, and which require more practice.

At some point, you'll need to use stories about data. Even if you don't regularly share data, you may want to work some into your stories. The next chapter explores the unique considerations for telling stories with data, building on the storytelling approach you've just learned.

SUMMARY

Make Everything Earn Its Place

See the checklists in the back of the book.

- Once you've built your story, validate you've effectively engaged the Five Factory Settings of the Brain. Use the checklist in the back of the book to identify what to add or remove.
- Go line-by-line through your story and ask yourself:
  - If this was cut, would anything be lost?
  - Does this create confusion?
  - Does this advance the story?
  - Should something be added or removed?
- Experiment with removing items and notice if the pacing or outcome is impacted.
- Ask yourself what you want your audience to know, think, do, or feel before potential interactions. This prepares you to tell stories in real-time.
- When telling real-time stories, use the four-part story structure to tell the story and work in one detail and/or engage one sense.

Peggy Fogelman
Norma Jean Calderwood Director, Isabella Stewart Gardner Museum

Who was Isabella Stewart Gardner, and what was her vision for the museum?

Isabella Stewart Gardner was a barrier-breaking, independent, no-holds-barred kind of woman. She lived through the Civil War, World War I, and many upheavals in American society. Isabella established the museum as an act of civic leadership and as her contribution to American society, intending to give people access to beauty who might not otherwise have it.

Isabella was very driven by the emotional and personal response to works of art. She wanted visitors to have a multisensory, aesthetic experience—smelling the flowers in the courtyard, hearing the trickle of water in the fountain, and seeing the exceptional collection of works of art.

How do you approach storytelling for the museum?

Isabella's will strictly dictated that the installation and works of art could not be permanently changed. We are a non-collecting museum. Our responsibility is to dig deeper to find meaning in these works of art that speak to our lives today. I find that very exciting.

There are so many stories within the museum: the individual objects, galleries, courtyard, and architecture. She wanted everyone to be able to form their own interpretation and not dictate the meaning or predetermine conclusions about a work. For example, according to her intention, there are no labels in the permanent galleries.

I think a lot about, *What is the DNA of this place that comes from her, and what potential does it have to inspire and enlighten us today?* For example, we did an exhibition called *Boston's Apollo*. It featured drawings made by John Singer Sargent in preparation for painting a mural on the rotunda of the Boston Museum of Fine Art. He was good friends with Isabella. She even lent him one of the galleries as a studio.

Our curator looked at these drawings in our collection and realized they all depict a specific Black man. We researched and learned he was Thomas McKeller, a young man living in Roxbury, Massachusetts. He modeled for Sargent for almost a decade and must have had a close relationship with him. He was clearly important to Sargent's work, yet he had been erased from the history of art.

We told this story of Thomas McKeller through the voices of community collaborators, shedding light on intentional and unintentional blind spots in telling history. It was an honor to make visible something and someone who had become invisible but was very important to public art and the history of Black Boston.

In March 1990, thirteen pieces of art were stolen from the museum. How is that story told?

It's part of our history and is an active, ongoing investigation. We remain very optimistic the works will be returned. There are two aspects to that story. One is to keep the focus on the works of art themselves. Isabella intended these works for the public. It's a loss for the public, not just for the Gardner Museum. Keeping them in the public mind can only help the chances of them coming back to us.

The other is thinking about how you frame the idea of absence and loss. We can all relate to this question. We intentionally keep the empty frames in the gallery, both as a reminder of what has been lost and as a very poignant stimulant to the imagination.

THIRTEEN

Storytelling with Data

As the head of data analytics for a construction company, Lucas had years of customer satisfaction data. He kept running into obstacles getting his leadership team to view the data credibly or make data-informed decisions. He was met with comments like, "Customers are clueless. They don't know what they are talking about."

Over six months, customer satisfaction dipped from 70 percent to 20 percent. There were too many quality issues that could no longer be overlooked. But instead of pulling up a slide with the data, Lucas started the next biweekly quality meeting differently.

"I was just reading an article about a woman named Trish who recently got back from a cruise. She had been planning this dream vacation for years, saving up thousands of dollars to bring her eighty-one-year-old mother, two sisters, and their children. The eleven family members went on this two-week cruise from Miami, through the Panama Canal, all the way to Los Angeles.

"Once they were settled onboard, Trish and her kids went to the pool, decked out in their bathing suits and neon green goggles. But before they could lay their towels down, they came face-to-face with yellow caution tape and a 'Pool Closed for Renovations' sign. They were baffled why the cruise line didn't complete this before the ship was underway.

"In a few hours, they realized this wasn't a vacation: it was a floating construction site. Several sections of the ship were blocked off with 'Under Repair' signs and yellow tape. Thick dust coated entire sections of the rails and floors. The workers wore protective respirators. Guests put towels over their heads when they went outside to avoid breathing in dust or getting it in their eyes.

"Echoes of equipment grinding, cutting, sanding, drilling, and hammering bounced off the side of the ship. Construction debris began drifting over to passengers. Chemical fumes could be smelled inside the ship from the varnish they were using to resurface decks. The smell was so strong, it made their nostrils curl. Some passengers ended up in the infirmary—only to later learn they were charged for the visit."

At this point, Lucas's team began saying, "That's insane! They deserve a refund."

Lucas holds his hand up and says, "It gets worse. Five hundred passengers gathered in the dining room to confront the captain midway through the trip. They felt they were blindsided, duped, and their health was at risk. They asked many times, 'Why weren't we told at booking or offered a discount?' The captain started listening compassionately. But he grew frustrated as the conversation went on.

"Then . . . he walked out.

"Passengers took to social media, documenting what was happening. Their attorneys filed complaints with the corporate office of the cruise line. They requested refunds, citing the passengers never would have booked the cruise had they known the boat's condition.

"The corporate office sent apologies to the passengers, acknowledging they didn't meet expectations or the company's standard. A 50 percent discount on future bookings was offered. The passengers were livid. They blasted the cruise line again across social media. Only then did the corporate office realize their mistake and offer each passenger a free cruise, valid for one year."

Lucas paused a minute to let the story sink in. It didn't take long for his team to react.

"Who would book another cruise with them?"

"That is terrible treatment!"

"If that was me, I'd sue."

"You can't treat customers that way and expect to keep them!"

Lucas sat quietly as different people around the table called out why they thought the cruise line was wrong. Then he leaned forward and pressed a button on his laptop.

A video of a man began to play on a screen at the front of the room. Greg introduced himself as a customer of the construction company. He described saving for years to be able to afford a custom-built home—a dream for his family. But he didn't expect that dream to turn into a nightmare. On his closing date, he learned the home wasn't finished as his family moved in. No one had told him. The home was dirty, plumbing wasn't properly connected, and appliances were missing. He couldn't get a straight answer on how long it would take to be resolved. His family had to live in a construction zone for months when they were promised a finished home. He was somber and emotionless as he described his circumstances. He ended with, "You lied to me, and I trusted you. You lied to me and let me move into a home that wasn't finished."

The recording ended, and the room was still. Each person realized the point of the cruise story. Lucas connected them to the emotions of an unfair customer experience so they couldn't ignore their own. He helped them see things they could no longer unsee.

Lucas cleared his throat and said, "When we ask our customers for feedback, they have the option to voluntarily record a video of their experience. And we have other examples just like this one." He then flipped to a slide to walk through the latest customer satisfaction data.

The story of the cruise helped connect the team to Lucas' takeaway idea: customer data should be explored, not discounted. Lucas helped them experience the frustration behind their customer data with a story from a different context. For the first time, the team listened and discussed the customer data without dismissing it.

DATA MYTHS

Earlier, I mentioned that people often don't think to combine stories and data in business. Our instinct is to favor data over stories. However, it isn't an either/

or decision. Stories connect your audience to the data. They create a shared understanding of the data, leading to better insights, discussions, and decisions.

One of the most common reasons people don't use stories in business is because they feel the unspoken norm is to only present data and that there isn't a place for stories. But data doesn't change our behavior—emotions do. Countless research has found drinking coffee to be both beneficial and harmful to our health. Yet the data doesn't persuade our habits. We drink coffee because we love the caffeine jolt or the daily ritual. Or we avoid it because we hate the taste or how it makes us feel. Our emotions guide our choices and actions.

There is a myth that data is fact and that it will do more to convince a listener than a story. We know from neuroscience research that we make decisions based on emotions, not logic. Data never speaks for itself. When you don't guide someone through data, our Factory Settings kick in. Our brains make assumptions and categorize information based on our experiences. The challenge is that we may come away with different interpretations. Our conclusions differ based on our experiences.

We live in a data-rich era with more insights, patterns, and even predictions of behavior from data each day than ever. We are also increasing our data savviness. Companies are learning how to be data-informed versus data-driven. Teams are figuring out how to avoid over-rotating on every piece of data.

I've spent many hours in meetings where data was mind-numbingly reviewed line-by-line. Instead of discussing insights or what actions to take, the conversation turned into a debate. *Do we trust the data or the source? Is the data from a representative sample? Do we agree on the interpretation?* The lack of trust and defensiveness over the data makes you wonder why it is even being collected.

A podcast host once said to me, "Some people avoid telling stories because data can be shared quickly. Stories require work." Just because it's easy to share information quickly doesn't mean the audience understands or remembers the data. The experience of the presenter often doesn't align with that of the audience. The presenter often is the owner and analyzer of the data, deep in understanding its nuances. The audience isn't as close to it and needs guidance to be able to understand it. Thought and effort are required to effectively bring the audience along toward what you'd like them to know about the data, or you end up with different interpretations. You can't have a meaningful discussion about data when everyone has a different understanding of it.

> Combining storytelling with data
> can bring that data to life.

I worked with a leader who once said, "Simple data leads to complex conversations." When the data is easy to understand, people have rich conversations about the considerations, insights, and decisions. When it isn't easy to understand, people debate its validity or interpretation. The trust of the person sharing the data is often called into question. Instead of awareness, confusion is created, defeating the point of collecting the data in the first place. Enter storytelling.

Combining storytelling with data can bring that data to life. The story provides a common understanding and starting point for discussion, even if there are different perspectives in the audience. This leads to a productive discussion instead of a debate.

WHEN TO TELL STORIES WITH DATA

Every presentation and piece of data doesn't require a story. However, the problem usually isn't in overuse. It's in *not* using stories with data frequently enough. Stories help bring meaning to data by framing it in a context the audience is familiar with and cares about. Storytelling may not be needed for a standing weekly meeting to review metrics. But many situations would benefit from sharing stories about data—depending on the desired outcome.

Help Connect to Deeper Understanding,
Mindset Shift, or Exploration

Lucas used the cruise line story to create a mindset shift. He needed the team to explore customer insights data. His story allowed the group to connect with a different perspective. If you have a team that is stuck in a pattern or is defensive, combining a story with the data can result in a different understanding. Even when the story is about a different topic than the data.

When You Have a New Audience

If you have a new team member, stakeholder, or decision-maker, tell a data story. Ground them in the understanding of why you're gathering the data, what's been learned to date, and what you are still exploring. Share what has been unexpected and validated. This not only level sets the new person with the rest of the group, but it also prevents incorrect assumptions.

Reaching a Decision/Milestone

As you approach decisions or milestones, share a story to help frame the decision. A story connects the audience to what they need to see and feel to decide. These stories often include one or two data points that support the takeaway of the story and don't involve pages of data. Supporting data can be kept in an appendix for reference if needed.

Insights Identified in the Data

David is the head of data analytics in a Fortune 500 tech company. I was helping him use storytelling to bring meaning to the monthly dashboard he reviewed with the leadership team. As David dug into the retention data, he noticed something unexpected: Managers, particularly women, were resigning at a higher rate than was normal for their industry. This career level often coincided with the point in people's lives when they were starting families and needed more flexibility. While the attrition data was within a normal range for the overall company, it spiked when it was broken down by career level.

Instead of starting with data at the next meeting, I helped David prepare to tell the story of Thais. She was a top-performing manager who left the company three months after returning from maternity leave. She was frustrated by the lack of flexibility and felt like she ran out of options. David then showed the retention data for managers across the company. Previously, the leadership team reviewed the number at the company level without comment. This time, they had a rich discussion of what they could do to support and retain managers. The story helped them recognize a larger problem that could be solved.

When you have data with outliers, unexpected outcomes, or patterns, tell their story to align the audience. The stories become the starting point for discussions and decisions.

To Understand Scale

Charities often tell you the story of one person. The Red Cross tells the story of one person or family whose lives were impacted by a disaster. You see their home destroyed and learn of their struggle to get food, water, and clothing. The weight of their loss becomes real, and your heart goes out to them. They then zoom out and help you understand the scale of the disaster and number of people impacted. The full size and scope of the problem lands differently. You now recognize the amount of help and support needed for those impacted. It's too hard to connect to the scale of something until you connect with it individually. Stories allow you to feel the scale of your topic.

HOW TO APPROACH STORYTELLING WITH DATA

In business settings, many people present too much data and create confusion based on the belief that the more data you share, the more credible you are. But *more* isn't better. More is *more* information to sort through. The person presenting the data has the responsibility to create understanding for others. That isn't done by sharing every piece of data collected. A few points are needed to support the takeaway and desired outcome—not a ream of paper. Stories connect the audience to necessary data with a handful of points.

Data is about people, situations, problems, and impacts—each of which are connected to emotions. Bring those emotions into the story. Talk about them before ever sharing the data. Ground the audience in the idea that the data informs—or questions for the group to explore. Stories help you connect people to an idea and support it with data.

Start with the Problems You Are Trying to Solve

Telling stories with data begins in the same place as regular stories: define the audience and desired outcomes to frame up the problems you are trying to solve.

1. Frame Your Problem Statement

Ideally, define this before you begin collecting data. What problem are you trying to answer, explore, or decide with the data? How will you use the data? Frame this problem statement as a question. Use it to align with your audience on the purpose and use of the data.

Example: *How might we increase retention across each level?*

2. Define the Type of Decision

Data can help inform different types of actions or decisions. Consider your problem statement and determine what action is needed.

- One-time decision: *What is happening?*
- Ongoing monitoring of trends and identifying outliers: *Why are these things happening?*
- Forward-looking, predictive, or informing strategy: *What might happen in the future? What should we consider next?*

Example: *Retention data is monitored on an ongoing basis for patterns, trends, or outliers. It's reviewed to understand what is happening and explore if adjustments should be made.*

3. Define Your Audience

Who is the audience reviewing the data? What is their current understanding of the problem statement? What is one thing you want them to know, think, feel, or do because of the data? What are potential obstacles in their understanding? These same questions from the storytelling framework help you make the data story relatable to your audience's understanding.

Example: *Retention data will be shared with Business Unit Leadership and HR. They're aware of attrition at the Business Unit level, but not by career level.*

- **Know:** *Attrition percentages by career level.*
- **Think/Feel/Do:** *Recognize when the numbers are approaching a concerning percentage and explore interventions.*
- **Obstacle:** *Not recognizing when the number is becoming concerning.*

4. Define Your Recommendation

As you analyze the data, what do you see? What insights does the data provide? What is important to know about the data? What is surprising or unexpected? What are your recommendations for the data: are you informing a discussion or decision? What are specific questions that will help guide the discussion or decision (if different from your problem statement). Guide your audience to their role in the process.

Example: *The retention data at the company and business unit level are within the industry average of 10 percent. When broken down by career level, it jumps to 19 percent for managers. This is often the stage in life when people are starting families and wanting flexibility. Recommendation: discuss how to support employees to bring the manager retention data within the industry average.*

5. Define the Smallest Amount of Data

What is the smallest piece of the data you can share to inform your problem statement and recommendations? How will you connect your audience to the smallest piece of data so they can understand the challenges and pain points, then expand to how big the problem is at scale?

1. What is the smallest piece of data you can share: such as a person, team, or project?
2. Within that data:
   1. What problems do they face?
   2. What pain points do they experience?
   3. What happens if something is or isn't done?

Example: *Thais is a manager who has been a top performer for three years. She returned from maternity leave three months ago. She recently resigned, citing* *burnout and frustration over the lack of flexibility. Thais is one of many managers struggling with similar challenges. The attrition percentage is already high and could continue to climb if different approaches aren't considered.*

Identify an Idea for the Data Story

Once you've answered the questions, resume the storytelling process. Choose the best story idea to connect your audience to the meaning of the data.

Do You Want to Tell a Story About the Data?

When you tell stories about the data itself, tell the story of the smallest piece of data possible. The story helps connect the audience to what was expected, what happened, and what they should consider or discuss.

If your data is about a group of 1,000 people, tell the story of one person before expanding to describe the impact for the full thousand.

Do You Want to Tell a Parallel Story?

Parallel stories connect the audience to an emotion or theme around the data by telling a story from a different context. You may use this when you have a defensive audience, controversial topic, or not enough firsthand knowledge about the data to mine a story. Lucas used a parallel story of the cruise ship to connect his company to the emotions of poor customer experience and to make them open to exploring their own customer satisfaction data. It's often easier to tell a story that is not related to the data. The audience focuses on the story and doesn't get hung up on data. Parallel stories can work well to create a different perspective or mindset shift.

Build the Data Story

Data stories follow the same story structure as regular stories. Write sentences for each of the four steps below to create the structure for your data story:

1. **What is the context?** What is the problem statement you set out to solve?
2. **What is the conflict?** What are you seeing in the data? What is unexpected or surprising?

3. **What is the outcome?** What is the impact? How does the data inform the problem statement?
4. **What is the takeaway?** What is the recommendation? What happens if nothing is done?

Follow the storytelling model to build out the story, including the emotions associated with the data. Help the audience feel the frustration with a problem. Connect them to the aspiration of what is possible. Let them experience annoyance that a problem is reoccurring. Surprise them with the unexpected items learned. Create discomfort by describing what happens if nothing is done.

Determine the best sequence for your data story. If you're telling a story about the data, you may want to start with the problem statement you set out to solve. Walk the audience through the problem you set out to address. Ground them in the initial questions you had, the journey you took, and what you learned and recommend. Anticipate challenges by sharing what is still unknown and being explored. If you're telling a parallel story, start there to connect the audience to the emotions and theme before sharing data.

When storytelling with data, the story provides the context and meaning. The data supports or reinforces the idea or takeaway. This is why you don't need forty-five slides; you likely need three data points to address the problem statement. The goal is to guide your audience to a shared understanding of the data to support decisions or dialogue.

Data stories leverage the same Five Factory Settings as regular stories. You want to build tension, slow assumptions, and connect the data to what the audience understands, all while connecting them to the emotions of the data to inform actions and decisions.

Visualize the Data

Data visualization approaches could be an entire book by itself. The way you visualize the story of your data will impact how it is understood. Data visualization comes only *after* you've identified the story of your data. Any visuals should support both the story you tell and the few data points shared.

Software and applications allow you to show different views of data during analysis from interactive spreadsheets to charts and graphs. When telling the story of data, you may want to present it outside of these applications. You don't need to show every data point—just the few reinforced in your story and recommendation. Keep detailed charts and graphs as a reference in an appendix, available for support as needed.

Focus on one idea per page. Most data visualization includes complicated charts and graphs. The voice-over dialogue is typically "I'm not going to read this to you" while the audience tries to make sense of what they are seeing. The more complicated the image, the less the audience listens to what you say. Simplify the visuals to share one idea to ensure your audience reaches the same understanding.

Guide your audience through the process. Take your audience on the journey of your data. Instead of starting with takeaways and recommendations, tell them the questions you had at the onset of the data gathering and analysis. Guide them through what was learned. Share what was unexpected and where you end up. Take them on the journey, and help them reach the same common understanding.

Don't default to charts or graphs to tell the story. The simpler the visual, the faster the understanding for your audience. Charts or graphs with multiple data points take time for your audience to orient themselves to, process, and figure out what they're to take away. Instead, remove the cognitive lift with visuals that convey a single piece of information like infographics, single sentences, or percentages.

Tell a story with descriptive takeaways as headers. Anytime you use a visual aid while presenting, like a slide, chart or graph, your audience will either listen to you or read the image. Only one wins, and it's usually the image. Use descriptive headers with takeaways to facilitate quick understanding. They should tell a story, building on the previous slides. This not only helps with faster comprehension, but it also ensures someone reviewing the presentation on their own reaches the same understanding.

Storytelling with data creates common understanding for your audience to support decisions or discussions. While it may take more time to prepare on your end, your audience benefits. Instead of debating validity, there are data-informed discussions about decisions and actions. Don't analyze if you should tell stories or share data. It's both. Together, they create a power ballad, dynamically connecting the audience to information.

There are two ways to influence the experience of a story: how it is constructed and how it is shared. The way you use your voice, gestures, expression, and pacing all impact the experience of the story. The next chapter helps you plan how to incorporate your body and voice when telling stories.

SUMMARY

Storytelling with Data

See the checklists in the back of the book.

- Data never speaks for itself. When you don't walk someone through data, you risk different interpretations and misalignment.
- Simple data leads to rich conversations. Make the data easy to understand and act upon. Stories help create simple data.
- Not every situation requires storytelling with data. Tell stories:
  - To connect to deeper understanding, mindset shift, or exploration.
  - When you have a new audience or stakeholder.
  - When approaching a decision or milestone.
  - To highlight insights and outliers in the data.
  - To understand scale.
- More data isn't better. More is more and confuses the audience. You are likely closer to the data than the audience and need to help them understand it. The data you include helps build a desired outcome for your audience.
- When telling stories with data, work through the storytelling process (see the checklist in the back of the book):
  - Define your problem statement.
  - Identify the type of decision to be made.
  - Define your audience.
  - Describe your recommendation.
  - Identify the smallest piece of data to share.
- Storytelling and data can either be a story about the data itself or a parallel story that connects to the idea and recommendation for your audience.
- Guide your audience through the data visualization to prevent confusion and misunderstanding.

Serena Huang, PhD
Global Head of People Analytics

What have you learned from spending your career leading and building analytics organizations?

I frequently talk about data insights with people new to analytics. There are very few conversations I have that don't involve data. The way you share the information makes a difference. Early in my career, I made the rookie mistake of starting with data. I thought it would bring me credibility. If you have a table with the numbers, delta variances, and benchmarks, then the conversation often ends as a debate about the numbers. Frame the data with the story and questions, and it is a different dialogue.

How do you incorporate storytelling with data?

Presentations today are data-rich but insight poor. Stories provide context to get to actionable insights. I begin with the desired mindset shift for the audience by asking, "What are we trying to solve?" I look for what may be tough to digest and where unexpected insights can lead to faster action.

I experiment with storytelling and data. I note what the audience cares about and see what resonates. My teams practice the elevator drill: sixty seconds on an elevator with a C-suite member to share what you've been working on. The rule is: any data shared has to be actionable or it's cut. Then we expand to five- or ten-minute versions, only allowing those things that are actionable.

What do people get wrong about storytelling and data?

Only sharing what is interesting to yourself. Start with the audience in mind. I look at the data and ask myself, *What decision will the data help inform?* and *What actions can be taken with this?* If the answer is *Nothing*, then it doesn't make it into the slide, presentation, or email. I'm also mindful to tell a balanced view of the data. You can't only tell the rosy perspective. You have to tell the bad or unexpected parts and recommendations. I also avoid sports stories and analogies to be inclusive globally.

The most important result is for action to be taken on data. Too much information can lead a sense of overwhelm and paralysis. Your audience won't always have the data acumen or time to get to the conclusion. Each slide containing data needs to clearly summarize the takeaway ("so what") and have a call to action ("now what").

How do you use visuals to tell the story of data?

Data visualization comes last to reinforce the story. I challenge my teams to make dashboards and charts in gray scale. Multiple colors are distracting and can emphasize too many points. In gray scale, black is used sparingly for emphasis. We also use a minimum font size for easy scanning and limited words. I've also studied research that people prefer circles and visually pleasing images. They help minimize resistance when there are difficult messages.

What advice would you give about storytelling?

Data analytics degrees aren't required! Some of the best data storytellers I've seen have no background in the field. It requires someone who can evoke emotions using data. The emotion the audience feels is what creates the action and change.

PART FOUR

The Outcome

Telling a Great Story

FOURTEEN

Telling Your Stories

The story about Maria and Walt began as most of my stories do: in writing. It's how I best work through ideas. I'm often not able to make sense of a story until I write it out. It started as a blog post three years before I told it on the TED stage. A few months after posting it, a podcast host unexpectedly asked me to tell it during an interview. I hadn't told the story live at this point and wasn't sure how to do it! Listing the events wouldn't do the story justice. I wasn't sure how to embody Maria or Walt when describing their stories. I hadn't thought about how to use inflection or when to vary my pitch, pacing, or pauses to make the story dynamic. The way you write a story on paper may not be the way you tell it. What works in one format may not work in the other. Stories need adaptation in either direction to make them compelling.

Written stories rely on your descriptions and details to engage the audience. The reader experiences pacing through varied plot points and sentence lengths. Short sentences with white space around them create pause. We get to be inside the head of the characters as we read their thoughts and emotions. The words do the work.

CONSIDERATIONS FOR TELLING YOUR STORIES

When you tell a story, you become a character as the narrator. Your speaking cadence helps to build and release the dramatic effect and tension. The audience is drawn into the story through your pace and vocal inflection. Pauses help ideas to land in their brain. With each pause, the audience feels what is said, and they experience emotions. Your gestures and facial expressions can demonstrate the emotions of characters without using words. When you tell a story live, the audience experiences it not only from what you say but how you say it with your body and voice.

Starting Your Story

"Let me tell you a story," Adam said.

"Hold on," I interjected, making the time-out sign with my hands. "Don't start there. You don't need to announce you're starting with a story. Just start telling it."

Adam was the CEO of a medium-sized tech company whom I'd been coaching for an upcoming presentation. Like many, Adam wasn't sure how to start the story.

"Isn't it awkward and confusing to start with the story?" he asked.

"Not at all. It's attention grabbing, which is exactly what you want."

People often begin stories by announcing them with phrases like "Let me tell you a story," "Let me set the scene," "Here is what happened," "Let me tell you about the time," and "Storytime!"

Don't do that.

> Comedians don't announce, "Now I will tell you a joke." They launch right into the joke.

You don't need permission. "Let me tell you a story" is the fastest way to make someone stop listening. It's as if your brain says, *"Oh yeah? Capture my attention, I dare you!"* as it slides into lazy mode. Jumping into the story is unexpected. Curiosity is created and makes the listener wonder what comes next.

Comedians don't announce, "Now I will tell you a joke." They launch right into the joke. You are right there with them every step of the way. The same is true for your stories.

This also applies to the details in your story. Don't include statements like "Let's call her (insert name)." Your audience doesn't care that a name in your story is made up to keep someone anonymous. These phrases steal attention.

Same goes for qualifying statements like "I don't know if this is any good." Just start—don't impact your audience's judgment. Anytime you find yourself wanting to use narration cues in the story, question if they add anything. In most cases, they don't. Tell the story. Name the characters. Your audience will track with you.

Brandon Stanton created *Humans of New York* as a website and series of social media accounts that tell stories of people around the world. He first started with a single photo of a person and a brief caption. He's evolved into posting a series of photos and captions that tell the story of one person. These begin at a moment of conflict for the individual without setting context.

One of his popular posts was a photo of a woman wearing all green clothing and the caption, "I found I was happiest in green, so I've been green for 15 years." You are immediately hooked and want to know more—why green? Why does wearing green head-to-toe make her feel happy? How did wearing other colors make her feel? Through each post, you learn more about the person and their story. You're intrigued by dropping into the conflict and learning as it progresses. Your audience wants a great story—not qualifying statements.

Use Your Body

Have you ever watched a graphics facilitator? These artists translate words into real-time visual icons and drawings. They keep up with the speaker, drawing the perfect graphics that visually represent what is said. They can do this because they have a vocabulary of images. If the speaker says "idea," they know to draw a lightbulb. The word "thinking" may result in the image of a brain. "Physical" could be drawn as a barbell. Each graphic artist has their library of images for the topic. They prepare in advance to make sure they can reinforce key concepts and words with planned images.

When you tell stories, have a library of gestures prepared. Use your arms, torso, and facial expressions to dynamically represent what is happening in the story. Plan intentional movements to demonstrate senses, emotions, and thoughts that reinforce your message. The movement also helps to dissipate nerves you may experience speaking in front of a group.

In storytelling workshops, I often have participants physically demonstrate their favorite emojis. We choose keywords from each of their stories to practice different movements. It's like a game of charades. Telling stories isn't just sharing the words. It's planning the movements that support them. Anything that depicts details, senses, or emotions is reinforced when you incorporate movement. Every word doesn't need an associated gesture. But major pieces of your story should have them.

Lindsey Saley was a grad student at Stanford when she discovered forward motion during moments of anxiety or amplified alertness cause the brain to release dopamine. It's like your own personal reward for being courageous. Gesturing, leaning, or stepping forward can give you this dopamine bump. It also builds motivation and reinforcement for you to tell stories again. Plan movements with forward motion not only to make your storytelling dynamic but also to get some free dopamine hits.

In my TED Talk, you can see me step forward and mimic pushing the button in the elevator to depict Maria's actions. I drop my hands to demonstrate the phone falling. My hand is held up to the side to demonstrate where the elevator inspection certificate hangs. Each time I bring a new person into the story, you see me step in a different direction. As I describe back and forth dialogue, my hands move from one side to the other.

When I describe Walt failing the exam, I widen my eyes in shock and shame. Whenever there is a number, I hold up the corresponding number of fingers. The movement is intentional to bring the audience further into what I am saying. Sometimes my gestures illustrate something specific, like the brain. Other times they reinforce emotions.

When you tell stories, you are part of the story. Your body reinforces what is said and brings the audience further into the story. The movement also helps to calm your nerves. As you prepare to tell a story, define the movements you will intentionally use.

Pause

A few years ago, I played my flute as a fill-in for a church holiday concert. There were two services with the same program, music, and sermon. In the first service, the pastor described Christmas Eve in his home growing up: "The anticipation felt throughout the day. The hours creeping by with the hands on the clock moving in deliberate slowness. The delicious family dinner made by Grandmother, with warm, buttered rolls that would melt in your mouth . . ."

There was more to the sermon, but my brain had me seated at my family's holiday table. I pictured a room humming with holiday warmth and laughter. My loved ones were seated around an oval table with a circular centerpiece of evergreens, holly, and white twinkle lights. I could smell the rich, savory mashed potatoes, cranberry sauce, and roasted turkey. The words "warm, buttered rolls that would melt in your mouth" made me feel like I had taken a bite of that roll. I could feel the warm, chewy dough oozing with butter.

In the second service, the pastor told the exact same story, reading from the same script. But this time the experience was different. His pace was faster, almost twice what it was in the first service. There was no lingering on the hours moving slowly or the anticipation felt while waiting for the holiday as a child. The buttered rolls were mentioned so quickly they felt like an afterthought. As he hastily moved past them, I thought, "But they're missing the warm, buttered rolls melting in their mouth!" It was the same words, but a different experience.

The difference was in how it was told. Specifically, his use of pause. In the first service, his pace and cadence were slower. He would pause after each sentence, letting it land. In the beat between sentences, you would feel the anticipation of the day. The hands on the clock moving slowly. Hours creeping by. It helped you picture your own family gathered around the table. You could taste the delicious, warm roll melting with butter in your mouth. The second time, there were no pauses. The difference in the stories wasn't in the words. It was in how they were delivered.

Pause allows the words to sink in. It's also a pattern interrupt. When you pause, the listener's brain notices. It slows inner dialogue and assumptions. The moment of silence allows words to land. The audience feels emotions and experiences as their brain catches up. Pause is one of your greatest tools in storytelling.

Not all pauses are equal. Shorter pauses should be used between sentences or transitions. Significant pauses should be used to build tension, and after landing a point, idea, or unexpected event. A short pause may be one second. A significant pause might allow you to count "one-one thousand, two-one thousand, three-one thousand."

When I describe Walt's final exam, I included a significant pause after the sentence, "What is the name of the person who cleans this room?" This lets the audience process what I said and think, *Would I have known the answer?* It also builds tension as you wait to learn if he knew her name.

As you look to tell a story, identify where you will incorporate pauses. Include a significant pause to be brain friendly. Use them to build suspense. Let the pause give space to the experience of the senses and emotions described.

Pacing and Pitch

Pacing is the cadence of the story. Varying the pace keeps the listener interested. It builds tension. An increase in pace sends a subtle cue to the brain that something is about to happen, the same way John Williams increased the pace of those two alternating notes in the movie *Jaws*.

I often accelerate pace when I am building to an unexpected event or an idea I want to land. I get faster, more animated, and increase pitch and inflection.

Then I pause.

And I wait.

I let it sink in.

After I share the idea, I resume at a slower pace and lower pitch.

Changing the pace and pitch kicks the brain out of lazy mode and makes it wonder what's coming next. Each story has an arc of energy. Varying the pace, pitch, inflection, and pause contributes toward building that energy or slowly releasing it. Combined, they almost become a character in the story, helping you land ideas in more impactful ways.

As you prepare to tell your stories, consider when and where you will vary your pace. How can you combine pace with pause to let ideas land? How can you vary your pitch and inflection to indicate different emotions?

Dialogue

Stories with multiple people often include dialogue. This can be tricky to navigate as a storyteller. You don't want to confuse your audience. What works for one storyteller often doesn't work for another. Experiment with what feels comfortable and natural.

Different voices for each character. This is tricky and should be done sparingly. Never mock people, their race, their culture, or gender. If the voice or accent feels forced or unnatural, the audience will focus on you and not the story. Especially if you don't have a genuine accent. You will lose credibility with your audience. Instead, vary your pace, inflection, and even body movements and gestures to indicate when a different character is speaking in your story.

Incorporate movement. I cannot sustain different voices naturally. Instead, I use movement to express dialogue of different characters. I change directions, facing one way to deliver the words of one character and then facing the opposite way for the other with major sentences. If there is a lot of dialogue, it can look unnatural to shift for every sentence. The audience ends up looking like they're watching a tennis match. When using movement, your feet don't have to move. Shift your shoulders to face a different direction and indicate a different person.

Know Your Start, Transitions, and Ending

Some people feel most comfortable scripting out every word. Others prefer to think of a few key points they build the story around. Whether you create a script or an outline for your story, know your opening sentence, closing sentence, and any transition sentences. These let you start and finish strong with smooth transitions, no matter what happens.

I script stories as I develop them. Then I set the script down and have key points to make throughout the story. I want the stories to feel like a conversation and not a monologue. Stories are often told differently in each delivery. I always have three scripted sentences: my opening, closing, and any transitions. These enable tighter stories for the audience to follow.

Sometimes you will feel inspired to try something in the moment—do it. Trust those things that come up, whether that is talking at a faster pace, using a different gesture—or in my case, a loud stage whisper.

In the middle of the TED Talk, as I got to the sentence, "Your brain is wondering, *Where is she going with this?*" I felt the urge to try something I had never done in rehearsals. I decided to use a loud stage whisper for the sentence, *Where is she going with this?* Some members of the audience later commented that it caught their attention. When you are telling a story and feel the urge to do something, do it! You've done all the work to prepare the story. This is your intuition giving you further insight into how to make the story great.

Speaking Rituals

Athletes often have set rituals before they perform. Baseball players play specific songs as they walk up to the batter's box. Tennis players may bounce a ball three times before serving. Golfers often practice their swing a time or two. These habits remove nerves and physically prepare them to perform. Create your own ritual before you speak and tell a story. Whether you choose to listen to a favorite song, power pose in a corner, or wear a favorite watch, find what grounds you.

In the final moments before telling a story, there are two things left to do:

The first is to channel the energy of a child who is excited to show you something. When showing you their bedroom or a piece of art they created, children vibrate with excitement. It's a moment of sharing and connection. That is the energy and mindset you want to tap into when telling a story. Focus on the excitement of sharing an idea with your audience.

The second habit is to tell yourself, *Have a conversation.* This is the last thing I think before stepping on the stage for each keynote. Whether I've practiced a story once or fifty times as I did with my TED Talk, I want it to feel fresh and conversational. The audience should experience the story as if we are sitting across from each other having coffee. That helps me land into a conversational tone, relax into a friendly presence, and have fun with the audience.

Experimenting and testing are part of the storytelling process. With each step of the storytelling methodology, consider if the story progression feels compelling enough to continue to the next step. If it doesn't feel right, back up a step or two and refine the story until it does. The next chapter demonstrates how to take a story that has gone through the process and test how it resonates.

SUMMARY

Telling Your Stories

See the checklists in the back of the book.

- Don't narrate your stories and say, "Let me tell you a story." Jump right in.
- Create a library of gestures that intentionally support your story. Include gestures that are forward moving.
- Pause is a character in your story. Embrace it to build and release tension.
- Vary pace, pitch, and pause to ramp up or lower energy in the story.
- When using dialogue, indicate different characters by gestures or movement.
- Know your starting, ending, and transition sentences for a strong start and finish.
- If you feel inspired to try something in the moment—do it!
- Create your own storytelling ritual to ground you before you begin.
- Channel the energy and excitement of a child about to show you something. Have a conversation with the audience!

John Cushing

Anything But Footy *Audio and Podcast Presenter and
Producer, Former Head of News Operations for* Global

**What was your previous responsibility with the Royal Family as the
Head of News Operations for *Global* in London?**

I was the person responsible for communicating any British royal family death on all *Global* radio stations broadcasting across the United
Kingdom during Queen Elizabeth's reign. Royal deaths include week-long
observances and protocol. Everyone expected me to know how to lead
this flawlessly. My palace briefing was a single sheet of paper. I relied
on my experience, knowledge, and some assumptions. The responsibility
loomed, following me with each promotion.

The Queen's story was written for years, yet there were many possibilities for mistakes. I knew the way the story was told would completely
impact the experience of a nation. Journalists had gone their entire
careers without having to tell the story of a royal death or coronation.
This weight sat on my shoulders.

If I made a mistake, it would be the hallmark of my career. That was
quite sobering. I'd already spent years leaving meals early or cancelling
plans because of breaking news. I would go to bed and wonder if this
was the night I would get woken up by a call.

I brought others into the process. While I was still responsible, I knew
I could test thinking and validate actions to avoid mistakes. I spent a lot
of time thinking, *How do we tell the story, get the right tone, and convey
proper respect? How can we avoid mistakes that can impact the experience of the story?* My plan was to focus on the same question I seek
to answer in any story: What is going to capture the listener's attention
and keep them listening?

I moved on before the Queen passed away. The team at *Global* did a great job announcing, reflecting, and continuing the coverage across the ten long days between Charles being declared King and the Queen's state funeral. I received messages of thanks from former colleagues for the briefings, protocol, and groundwork I'd done. That meant a lot. I don't think we should ever see that kind of widespread prolonged coverage again.

How has your storytelling evolved as a podcast host?

I now co-host the *Anything But Footy* podcast. We tell stories from Olympic and Paralympic sports and what happens in the four years between. I love to tell stories of athletes who inspire kids to ask for their autographs.

Podcasts give time and let you talk to a specific audience. Storytelling becomes easier when you aren't focusing on mass appeal. Just as I did in the news, I believe in keeping interviews tight and bright. Go longer than you should, and the audience switches off.

Where news journalists are in search of headlines, our podcast creates flowing conversation with thoughtful questions. The more interviews you do, the better you get at listening. For me, that is the key thing as an interviewer. These interviews can become quite formulaic: "How are you feeling? What are you looking to achieve?" There is always a back story as to why someone is talking to you. Dig under the surface and get their story. Make the connection between them and the listener.

FIFTEEN

How Do I Know If My
Story Resonates?

I was three sentences into delivering my TED Talk when it happened. I had just said, "Her phone fell out of her hand, bounced on the floor, and *whoosh*! It went straight down that little opening between the elevator and the floor."

In the second row of the audience, someone gasped and exclaimed, "No way!" It was so loud that everyone in the front of the theater heard. I pushed down laughter and willed myself to keep going with a straight face. Inside, I was jumping up and down because I knew my story worked, and the audience was hooked.

I am often asked how I know a story will work. I don't. I learn by testing it with different audiences. Testing stories helps me see what resonates. It also puts a spotlight on the parts of the story I haven't figured out how to tell smoothly. I can immediately see if everything has earned its place, or if something creates confusion.

SIGNALS OF A GREAT STORY

Each story you tell is made up of two versions: the one you tell and the one received by the audience. Each person will listen to a story and have their own interpretation based on their experiences. I learn what the audience experiences through testing stories. Often, these are the moments that give me ideas to make the story more meaningful.

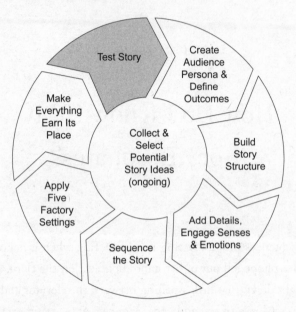

The Physical Effect

I frequently give keynotes for corporations and conferences. Occasionally, I will guest lecture at universities. One of my first guest lectures was for Purdue University on storytelling. I found myself looking at the tops of students' heads as they bowed over laptops taking notes. I opened with a story and immediately had a hundred pairs of eyes glued on me. Everyone leaned forward and sat frozen as if I used a stun gun on them. As I finished the story, heads lowered as they quickly typed their thoughts. This talk had about twelve different stories throughout it. Each time, the same thing happened. Typing stopped, heads lifted, and they listened while frozen.

There is often a notable physical response during stories. The audience stops what they're doing, leans forward, and stays motionless. Take note of your audience when you're telling a story. What are they doing? Are people looking at you? Are heads nodding? What is the physical shift you notice as you tell a story?

Don't fret if your audience isn't looking at you. Often, your story will prompt their own thoughts and recall of experiences. You may notice them looking up and to the side as they reflect. They may drift off for a moment to think—which is a great thing! An audience that has lost interest altogether often stares blankly or becomes slouched in their body language. Notice the difference between when you've triggered thoughts for your audience or lost their interest altogether.

The Pattern Interrupt

I was designing and facilitating a leadership retreat for a C-suite team. This Fortune 500 healthcare company was stuck working in silos. They were quick to blame and slow to trust and collaborate. Miguel, the CEO, was beyond frustrated with their performance. He was skeptical the retreat could unpack and resolve their challenges.

Miguel and I met to begin planning the workshop. I quickly realized I was being tested. Each time I tried to discuss the retreat or the agenda, he would interrupt with a question. He wanted to gauge my ability to handle a difficult group and have tough discussions. Each interruption was a challenge to see if he could trust me.

"The team complains that I've set unrealistic revenue goals. Do you think I should lower their revenue targets?" he asked.

Miguel didn't need my input on whether he should lower targets. He was assessing my understanding of the team. I had been around them enough to know their challenge wasn't revenue targets, it was in their overall interactions. I felt there was a perspective Miguel wasn't considering: his role in the team dynamics.

"You ran track in high school and university, right?" I asked Miguel.

"Absolutely, made it to State three out of four years," he replied.

"Fantastic! How often did you get to set your target pace for each race?"

Miguel started laughing. "Never. Coach decided it, and I had to make it happen."

"When you went to practice, did your coach ask you how you were feeling? How you had slept? What were you eating? Did he suggest how to tweak your training plan based on your responses? Was he ensuring you had adequate recovery time? Did he coach you to help you achieve your goal? Or did he give you the goal and let you figure it out yourself?"

Miguel got quiet and looked at me, slowly nodding his head.

I then said, "What if you coached the team more—regardless of their goals? Could you engage them in discussions to figure out what is needed? Are there obstacles you can help remove? Can you suggest tweaks to guide performance, just as your coach did?"

I used Miguel's experience to connect him to a story that was familiar to him. One that served as a pattern interrupt to make him open to our discussion.

> Stories can disrupt behaviors or
> conversations that are stuck in a loop.

He stopped testing me and said, "I see what you're getting at. You're right. I haven't been doing that enough. Let's talk about how to use this retreat to achieve that."

Stories interrupt patterns. They can disrupt behaviors or conversations that are stuck in a loop. They open a door for something different. They can change the energy in a discussion or on a team. Thinking can be expanded or new ideas embraced. Notice when stories cause a change in behavior, and intentionally use them as pattern interrupts.

Quoting You Back to You

"I hold my phone so carefully when I get into an elevator."

"My Dottie's name is Vincent."

"What was the brand of iPhone case that saved Maria's phone?"

You know a story resonates when someone in your audience recounts specific details of the story. People love to tell you their favorite pieces, like they're reciting lyrics to a favorite song. Asking people what stood out for them in the story indicates its resonance. If it didn't resonate, you'd get general or vague responses: "I liked it, it was good." Or, "That was different." When a story resonates, you get very specific examples of what they connected with. When testing your stories, ask, "What stood out to you?" Listen for specific details.

I See Your Story and Raise You a Story

How often have you heard someone tell a story that makes you think of a related story to share? When someone shares a story in response to yours, it means two things. First, your story resonated with them. It leveraged the Factory Settings by linking them to what they understood, and it reminded them of their own related experience. Second, it shows connection. We share stories of our connection to an idea, person, situation, or moment.

You know a story resonates when people tell you one in return. It is the unspoken "I see you, now I want you to see me." Take note of what anecdotes or stories are shared after yours. Ask, "What was it about my story that made you think of this?" These responses will help you understand what is valued and resonates most about your story.

A Show of Support

As I finished giving a storytelling keynote to a tech company, a small group gathered to talk with me. The first person said, "I just gained a new level of understanding for what compelled me to donate to an animal rescue earlier today. I wasn't asked to support homeless animals. They didn't even request a donation. They told a story about a specific dog. Before I knew it, I was clicking the 'donate' button."

Stories leave us feeling empathy and trust toward the storyteller. That often translates into a show of support through money, time, resources, or awareness. Notice the response of your audience. Do they verbalize support? Are resources committed? Do they offer help? Are there requests for additional information or follows on social media? Does your audience begin persuading others? Watch for the signals of support that show your story resonates.

Expanding and Shifting Thinking

I was facilitating an off-site meeting with a Fortune 500 media company's leadership team to define a new culture strategy. They kept suggesting incremental improvements to their current strategy that wouldn't address the challenges they faced.

I put up a photo of a penny-farthing, one of those bicycles from the late 1800s with a huge wheel in the front and a tiny wheel in the back. I told the story of the evolution of the bike, describing how the front wheel was made larger to increase speed. At a certain point, the wheel couldn't get bigger, the rider's legs weren't getting longer, and the bicycle couldn't go faster. A new design was needed to reimagine transportation—leading to the current bicycle design with two same-sized wheels connected by a chain. I connected the metaphor to the culture strategy. It was time for a new design that would lead to different results. This shifted their thinking. They discussed the current limitations of their culture strategy and defined a new approach.

A great story can help shape the ideas of your audience. There is often a notable shift in thinking, understanding, and discussions. Pay attention to the conversations after telling the story and note the willingness for a different dialogue.

The Room Where It Happens

The methodology for developing and telling stories is the same for in-person or virtual deliveries; however, there can be differences in how they are experienced. When told in-person, a shared energy may be created. It often doesn't translate through video or virtual connections with the same intensity. There can also be an energy shift felt in the room when the meeting is in person and emotions are intensified. A shared story can feel quite magical. There is a cumulative energy shift from the engagement of emotions and neural coupling. Notice when the room feels different after telling in-person stories.

Ask for Feedback

Whenever people connect with me after a talk, I ask them, "What stood out to you?" The responses differ by person, and it's always fascinating to hear. Ask specific questions to understand the experience. A question like, "What did you think?" will lead to the same response you get when asking a kid about their day at school: "It was good."

Probe for specificity. "What was good? What stood out? What did you connect with? What did you expect to happen? What would make it better? Where did the energy dip? Was there any spot where the pacing felt too slow? Was anything confusing? What surprised you?" It's often helpful to share, "This is a new story I am testing. What should I do differently when I tell it again?" Ask how well your story achieved the desired outcomes and what tweaks are needed.

MEASURE THE ENERGY OF YOUR STORY

Each story has an energy arc that ebbs and flows throughout. This fluctuation is normal and necessary. A story with a flat line of low energy will trigger the audience's brain to become lazy and tune out. Stories with a constant high level of energy may overwhelm and exhaust the audience.

When creating the story, be aware of opportunities to build and release tension with plot points and unexpected details. As you tell the story, amplify those points with gestures, pacing, pitch, and pause. As you practice, test the story to see if the energy variation and story arc are experienced as planned.

Plot the energy of a story on a graph. The bottom axis includes the key points of the story. The vertical axis indicates high, medium, and low energy. For each key point, indicate where you think the energy falls when telling the story. The following chart provides an example of the energy for Maria's portion of the opening story of my TED Talk.

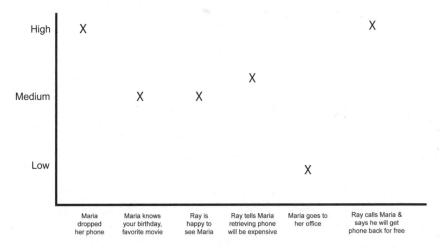

When testing your story, give different people a blank graph with labeled axes. Ask them to plot the energy level as you tell your story. I often start with someone I know and trust. Then I test the story on someone from the target audience. The graph helps me ask follow-up questions about their experience and takeaway.

The graph should show variation. Are the peaks and valleys where you expected? Do you need to vary your pace, inflection, or pauses? Does your story need to be told in a different order? Would the experience change if you added unexpected elements?

Test your stories to figure out if you have the right elements and order for your story. Gain insight into the audience response. Every story you tell may not need to be tested. The higher the stakes, the more time you want to plan and test your story.

Testing your stories can help you see where they go wrong. We all have stories that don't quite achieve what we hope. Often, they come from some common mistakes and patterns we overlook. Learn those patterns and how to avoid them in the next chapter.

SUMMARY

How Do You Know If a Story Resonates?

See the checklists in the back of the book.

- There are two stories: the one you intend and the one received by the audience. Your audience comes away from stories with their own understanding based on their own experiences.
- There are a few clues that your story resonates:
  - Your audience gives you physical cues: leaning forward, smiling, nodding heads, or even verbal responses.
  - The story acts as a pattern interrupt, changing the conversation or behavior that is stuck in a loop or script.
  - People quote parts of your story back to you.
  - Audience members tell you stories in return.
  - The desired outcome is achieved, or action is taken after the story.
  - Conversations expand to different ideas, considerations, and thoughts.
  - There is an energy shift felt in the room where the story is told.
- Ask specific questions to your audience like "What stood out to you?" These help you get deeper insight to their "I liked your story" and understand what truly resonated for them.
- The energy of each story ebbs and flows. It can be plotted to understand where tweaks may be needed to how the story is told. Practice plotting this during story development and testing.

Dr. Anthony Williams

Physician, Assistant Director of Center for the Art of Medicine,
University of Minnesota; Associate Program Director, Med-Peds
Residency Program, Health Partners Med-Peds Hospitalist

How does the Center for the Art of Medicine at the University of Minnesota Medical School incorporate storytelling?

We want to cultivate curiosity and creative expression in medical education and practice. Arts and humanities are not separate from science and scientific reasoning. They can help physicians and physicians-in-training be more resilient throughout their practice.

You tell a narrative or an emotionally charged story, and we are all there with you. Storytelling combats burnout and isolation by creating community. We do a very tough and draining job. It's challenging as a medical student and only gets more challenging as a resident and beyond. It's easy to feel isolated.

We teach medical students and residents how to tell stories. We also create community through events like Story Slams and Hippocrates Cafes that give hope and make you feel less alone. We have lots of Kleenex at these events. Even some of the happy stories can be bittersweet.

Our industry historically doesn't admit weakness, vulnerability, or mental health issues. That is the dark side of the rhetoric around "Healthcare workers are heroes." It's dehumanizing with good intent. We are people who have families and lives outside of medicine. We break, have trauma, and struggle with mental health issues. If we don't talk about it or share stories to feel community, then we burn out, commit suicide, and have a lot of other issues.

When someone is really nervous to tell stories, we start them writing with a sensory grid. We have the medical student think of a situation that is happy, sad, or emotionally charged. The grids has prompts: "What were the sights? The sounds? The smells? What did you taste? Who was there?" They aren't constructing a story; they are writing out lists.

That is perfect for a Type A medical student. Then they write a fifty-five-word story using the sensory grid. Usually, they like that and are able to construct a story they at first thought was impossible.

How do you use stories to relate to patients?

One of the things I teach medical students and residents is the ultimate arbiter of how the patient feels about your encounter and whether follow your recommendations is how you package the information.

Patients tell you how they think by the way they tell their story. An engineer may list out detailed data and the time of their problems. When I talk to them about recommendations, I will lay out the data the same way—very logical, very linear.

Many people will tell you about the responsibilities they couldn't fulfill because of what was happening. I then structure recommendations as, "I want you to take this medication so you can be alive for your granddaughter's high school graduation." Recommendations like, "Take this because it cures diabetes," don't really work to keep people understanding and invested in their care.

I change the clothing that my recommendations wear based on the type of stories I get from the patient. Stories are threaded all through the reception of patients, from what's going on with them to giving recommendations with rationale and reasoning.

SIXTEEN

Where Do Stories Go Wrong?

The first time I saw the Fearless Girl, I had just finished a half-marathon in New York City. I had run across Central Park, through Times Square, and down the West Side highway, crossing the finish line near Wall Street. After getting my medal and water, I began walking to cool down. My head was down, and I almost didn't notice her until we were face-to-face.

I stood looking at her for a good minute, my eyes unexpectedly welling with tears. She was a foot and a half shorter than I was, but her stature made her seem taller. Her expression was a mix of confidence, determination, and strength. I handed my phone to a woman next to me and asked if she would take my photo. I put my hands on my hips, squared my shoulders, and lifted my chin with a smile. It was a perfect mimic of her pose. My silent salute and nod to the girl. We looked nothing alike, but at that moment, I was her. She symbolized everything I felt crossing the finish line.

After taking the photo, the woman exchanged places with me. She gave the same silent salute, mimicking the same pose. As I took her photo, a tear tumbled down her cheek and over her smile. I stepped forward to hand her phone back and noticed a group gathering to take photos with the statue. I overheard a father tell his young daughter how important it was for women to be in leadership and have their voices heard. A pregnant woman rubbed her belly in circles, telling the woman next to her she hoped her daughter would grow up with the confidence and determination this figure symbolized. Three generations of women in a family posed for their photo. The grandmother put her arm around her granddaughter and said, "For you, it will be different."

The energy of the entire group was quiet and poignant. This wasn't a tourist spot; it was a pilgrimage each visitor wanted and needed to make. She was a symbol of hope and a vow for a different future. Many wiped away tears, surprised by the emotion that snuck upon them. The original intent of this sculpture no longer mattered. She represented millions of different stories for each visitor.

The Fearless Girl didn't start as an inspiring symbol of hope. She was almost a tragic mistake. State Street Global Advisors was launching a new fund under the ticker SHE. They wanted to create a buzz and bring awareness to gender diversity in leadership. After months of discussion, they settled on installing a statue. At the base would be a plaque with the inscription: *"Know the power of women in leadership. SHE makes a difference."*

The statue would represent feminine energy and a call for women in leadership. It would stand opposite the charging Wall Street Bull in defiance. After months of work, a design was made, plans were signed off, and permits were filed for *The Wall Street Cow.* That's right, the original design for a positive symbol of women in leadership was a life-size, bronze cow.

While obviously cringeworthy in hindsight, it's easy to recognize the initial thinking leading to the idea of placing a cow opposite the bull. It's plausible to forget about the audience and intent when you're excited by a concept and a design. It took eight months before the team realized that a cow might be demeaning to women. You can imagine how quiet and uncomfortable that conference room was as State Street Global Advisors and the advertising team recognized their mistake. The group pivoted to a statue of a young girl and got to work on new designs.

Just over four feet tall, the Fearless Girl statue took her place on the eve of International Women's Day in 2017. She stood staring down the Wall Street Bull with hands on her hips, skirt swooshing, and ponytail swinging. She defiantly raised her chin and brimmed with empowerment and confidence. Lines of people queued each day to imitate her pose and strength as they took a photo. This fearless girl was more than a symbol. She represented a personal story for each individual who stood beside her. As people shared their photos on social media, the lines grew daily.

> Storytelling doesn't have to be time-consuming, but it does require some preparation.

The original permit was for a one-week installation across from the Wall Street Bull. That one week turned into a month, then a year, until it moved to its permanent location across from Wall Street. The popularity of the Fearless Girl expanded internationally, with replicas installed in Australia, Norway, and England. Her popularity grew with each story shared on social media. She gained 4.6 billion Twitter impressions and 745 million Instagram impressions in just twelve weeks.

Stories often resemble the concept of the Wall Street Cow when they go wrong: the wrong idea, wrong audience, and wrong time. They don't land as hoped, leaving out crucial details and the audience scratching their head in confusion. Storytelling doesn't have to be time-consuming, but it does require some preparation. Work the steps, and you can create a great story. Skip steps, fail to prepare or plan, and your stories will fall flat. Or worse.

COMMON STORYTELLING MISTAKES

There is a big gap between telling a story and telling a great story that engages your audience. Shortchange the storytelling process, and your stories may stumble and falter. Most common mistakes can be avoided with awareness and planning.

Mistake 1: The Uncle at the Dinner Table

Don't tell the story you want to tell; instead, tell the story the listener needs to hear.

I almost gave a different TED Talk. While I had the idea for my talk, ironically, I was struggling with finding the right stories. There were so many

I wanted to include. Stories I've used in keynotes with a great response. Those that held personal meaning and joy for me. My most requested stories.

Each time I tried to fit one of these stories in, I felt like I was losing the idea. It was like I was looking through a camera lens that I couldn't bring into focus. This talk was taunting me. I couldn't figure out why.

There is a pattern to preparing a talk. You start excited to share your idea. It's like a Monet painting: lovely, a bit fuzzy, with the general idea discernible. As you put your ideas on paper, the questioning begins. You realize how out of focus things are. *Is this clear? Am I saying anything different? Am I even building an idea?* Next comes the phase where you hate the talk, wondering how you will ever pull it together.

Then the magic happens.

In this period of doubt, your brain focuses. You become ruthless about what stays and is removed. Which, in my case, came after a conversation with a friend who told me to "kill my darlings," as Sir Arthur Quiller-Couch advised writers over a century ago.

I was trying to force-fit these stories into the talk. They were ones I wanted to tell, but not the ones the audience should hear to build the idea. I was focusing on me and not my audience. As soon as I cut the stories, everything immediately became clear. I realized the elevator story brought the idea to life, and it became a different talk.

Sometimes we are so caught up in the act of telling a story, we forget all about the audience. Most of our communication intends to inform, influence, or inspire. If you don't start with your audience and define the desired outcome, your story will go wrong. Which makes you no better than the uncle at the holiday table repeating the same dreaded stories over and over. He repeatedly tells those stories for himself, not for you.

Ever see someone sharing a story that they love, only to have it fall flat? Or a story that seems pointless, or just doesn't make sense? Chances are that these stories focus on the storyteller and completely miss the audience.

When you prepare to tell a story, begin with the audience in mind. Each person filters the story through their understanding and experience. If you aren't starting with your audience and desired outcomes, the version you tell may have no relation to the version your audience understands. Meet them where they are. Tap into their emotions, beliefs, values, and mindset. Build the story to support the takeaway idea. Don't share a story that you want to tell. Build the story the audience should hear.

Mistake 2: The Spineless Skeleton

Don't neglect the structure of your story.

I met Todd a month before he was going to pitch for Series A funding for his startup. The first time we met, I asked him to take me through his pitch. For the next five minutes, I listened to a string of anecdotes about early customers. They were hard to follow and presented no specific takeaway. I couldn't understand the customers' problems or how the product solved them. His pitch was stream of consciousness with many confusing details. I felt my brain slowly wandering and checking out.

The opening story should have helped me build empathy for Todd's customers. I wanted to feel their frustration. He could have instilled a sense of hope about the different problems the product solved. I wanted to experience the same palpable relief as customers had using the product. Instead, I was left unsure who would use the product and why.

Todd's story was missing structure that created context, introduced conflict and tension, and demonstrated the outcomes and the takeaways. I wanted the structure to make it easier to guide my brain to the desired outcome. A story lacking structure is like a skeleton without a spine. It doesn't come together. It is shapeless and open to interpretation. The structure helps guide the listener through key details to ensure the audience lands on the desired outcome.

Mistake 3: Meaningless Details Stall Stories

Meaningful detail brings a story to life, but don't pile on irrelevant information.

In my storytelling workshops, I ask for a volunteer to share a story. No matter who volunteers or what story is told, the same pattern emerges. The person tells a story full of details that meant something to them, but not the audience. They get stuck trying to remember specific dates, locations, and sequencing of events that they lose the storyline and plot. Or worse, they go off on a tangent and start a second, completely different story. It's a bit like someone recounting a dream that was vivid and high stakes to them and meaningless to others. The flurry of insignificant details detracts from the story, making it hard to follow.

Details that aren't relevant to the story or don't move it forward give permission for the audience's brain to check out. When stories are so cluttered with details that don't matter, they steal space from the ones that do. Meaningful details engage senses, create tension, and move the action forward.

Details bring a story to life, make us feel something, and make the story memorable. There is a balance between too many and too few details. They must also earn their place. If a detail can be removed and nothing is lost, cut it. If the audience doesn't connect with your story, experiment with incorporating different details.

Mistake 4: Early Is on Time, on Time Is Late

Leave yourself enough time to craft and practice your story.

Each May, I expect my phone to ring with Rohan on the other end. He is the CEO of an international professional services company that I've worked with for years. Every June, Rohan brings together his top five hundred leaders for an in-person session that lays out the strategy and services for the coming year.

The first time Rohan and I worked together, he planned to announce a new strategy and direction for the company that expanded into new markets and clients. His presentation was going to challenge thinking. The problem was that Rohan reached out to me three days before he was due to present.

The presentation lacked structure and emotion. It was forty-seven pages of analyst data and charts. It needed a story to help the leaders get excited about the approach. They needed to see what problems their teams would solve and feel their clients' relief. Three days was a rushed timeframe to identify a story, restructure the presentation, test it, and have Rohan practice on top of everything else he was doing. I had Rohan clear his schedule, and we worked throughout those three days to get him ready. In the middle of the second day, Rohan said, *"I get it, I should have called you in early May."*

WHERE DO STORIES GO WRONG?

Most people spend hours preparing slides for a presentation and only leave five minutes to think about what they might say. Great stories aren't made up on the fly. They become great through iteration and revision. Leave time to create your story. Your best ideas often don't come until the third, fourth, or seventh revision, not on the first attempt. Successful stories require time to think of the idea, plan the structure, and practice.

Mistake 5: Lacking Emotion

Your audience won't connect to a story that lacks emotion.

A photo of the sun setting behind the office building filled the screen behind Jaime. She described how she was driving home a few nights before and pulled over to capture this beautiful sunset. To her, it was a symbol of all the changes and growth the company had experienced and of the opportunity ahead.

As she looked out into the audience, she was met with blank faces. She told a story! She even used a photo. Why did it fall flat?

She didn't bring her audience into the photo. There was no engaging of the audience's senses by describing the colors of the sunset, the way the air smelled, or how the building looked like a mirage. She didn't describe how frustration turned to pride as the company navigated so many changes, how the number and variety of those changes were reflected in the many colors of the sunset. She listed facts that told a flat story, devoid of feeling. Even two or three sentences that leaned into emotion could have helped her create a connection with the audience.

Storytelling is the original artificial reality: it lets us see, hear, feel, taste, and emotionally experience things we haven't encountered. Failing to engage the senses and emotions only limits our capacity for connection and understanding. The best stories invite you in, letting you experience the story firsthand, even if you have never been in that situation before.

Mistake 6: The Secret Keeper

Don't spend your energy on withholding information.

John is one of my writing mentors. His suggestions expand my thinking and help me see things I completely missed. He once said to me, "I could tell you were rushed when you were writing that leadership article about the Halloween costume. I feel like if you had more time, you could have made us feel like we were wearing that itchy costume and how it made us uncomfortable."

I started laughing and said, "I wasn't rushed. I was trying to avoid saying it was a French maid costume!"

I have recognized that when I am intentionally trying not to share something, I don't include enough of the right details and emotions. I often see leaders make this same mistake. The act of avoiding and withholding information they don't want to share makes them gloss over details they should. The energy that should go to creating the story is spent protecting information. The resulting story is flatter and less engaging.

One common place this shows up is in the characters of the story. Characters create conflict in stories and move the plot forward. We want to connect to their struggles, desires, discomfort, joy, or frustrations, as well as their impact on others in the story. Characters are often based on people from our life. There may be things we don't want to reveal about them. Holding back ends up diluting what makes characters relatable and dynamic.

Create your stories freely in the first pass. Include the characters, descriptions, and information you will later replace or cut. Build your story without holding back. Just as every detail earns its place, ask yourself, "Where can I expand details to bring the audience into this?"

Mistake 7: The Untested

Tested stories are perfected stories.

I was standing in a conference room in Spain. A room full of managers looked back at me with confused looks. I was in the middle of facilitating a leadership session and decided to tell a story based on a metaphor I had been thinking about for a few weeks:

Picture a plate of spaghetti. This is what your employees' brains feel like when facing changes. It's a jumbled mess. Now, picture a waffle. It's row after row of squares. You can focus on one at a time. This is your job as

a leader. Make waffles and not spaghetti for your employees. Help them
focus on what is important and ignore the rest.

As I told the story, I realized I had lost the audience. For a second, I wondered if it was because of a language barrier. But even after pulling up pictures of spaghetti and waffles, they were still confused. I hadn't tested my story in advance. It didn't work and needed refining.

A year later, I was back in the same conference room, this time with a larger group. I was facilitating a session on navigating changes. I decided to try a new version of the story I had prepared and tested many times.

I was working with a group of leaders who were facing change, just like
yourselves. As I looked around the room, I could tell they didn't want to be
there. Not because they didn't want to help employees, but from the sense
of defeat from past failures in implementing changes.

I decided to take a different approach with the group and said:
"Picture a plate of spaghetti noodles. They're a tangled mess that you
can't organize. Try to pick up one noodle and nine other strands are tan-
gled around it. If you do manage to get a single noodle free, it smacks you
in the chin while you eat. This jumbled mess of spaghetti is what your
employees' brains are like facing change. They're challenged to think
clearly and prioritize. At times, they feel like they keep getting smacked
by change.

"Your job as a leader is to make waffles for employees. A waffle
has row after row of neatly organized squares. You can focus on one
at a time and fill it with syrup or butter. You know the other squares
are there, but you don't pay attention to them until you're ready. Help
employees focus on what they can do and ignore the pieces they can't
control. Eliminate the noise and confusion to focus on what is needed
that day."

I knew I was onto something when the Italian in the group stood up
and said, "As much as this pains me, even I will make waffles and not
spaghetti."

As I finished, they said, "That's a great story! Why haven't you told it sooner?"

The elements of the story were the same. But through testing, I learned how to make it a great story. I realized I needed the audience to twirl the spaghetti, smell the waffles, and feel employee frustration. The metaphor of spaghetti and waffles connected them to the feeling of chaos and craving for structure. I figured out how to vary the pacing and pauses as I told it to hold their interest.

Ideas in your head often don't land as you expect when you share them. Leave space to test your stories. Use the feedback to refine not only the details of the story, but how you tell it for maximum impact.

When I tell stories that don't work, it always comes down to the same things: I didn't follow the process, or I rushed a step. I recognize it the moment I start the story and see it heading in the wrong direction. It's never a mystery why the story doesn't work.

One of the most important mistakes you want to avoid is having your audience feel like you're intentionally manipulating them. The moment your audience feels your story is manipulative or inauthentic, you lose them. The next chapter explores when storytelling becomes manipulation.

SUMMARY

Where Do Stories Go Wrong?

See the checklists in the back of the book.

- There is a big gap between telling a story and telling a great story that engages your audience. It's not enough to tell a story. The way you tell it impacts the connection with the audience and the likelihood of achieving the desired outcome.
- Common storytelling mistakes include:

  - Telling the story that you want to tell and not the story the audience needs to hear.
  - Neglecting to map out a structure for the story—making it hard for the audience to follow.
  - Including details that aren't relevant to the story or the audience.
  - Not leaving enough time to develop, revise, and practice your story.
  - Telling flat stories that don't connect you to any emotions or senses.
  - Focusing on what you don't want to reveal instead of what you want to include.
  - Not testing your story.

SEVENTEEN

When Does a Story
Become Manipulative?

I often hear the question: "Aren't you manipulating people by telling a story?" Can a story in the wrong hands be manipulative? Absolutely. Can data be manipulative? Absolutely. A story or data can be shaped to make any point. However, you aren't manipulating each time you communicate with a story or data. Communications fall along a continuum, with sharing information at one end and manipulation at the other. Somewhere in the middle are influence and persuasion.

We each have a desired outcome when we communicate—even when telling stories in social settings. There is always a takeaway we want for our audience. We often seek to inform, influence, or persuade someone to act—whether sharing information, data, or telling a story.

This is the reason the storytelling process begins with your audience and the desired outcome. The outcome helps you set an intention. The information we share and the way we connect the audience to it determines whether that message is influential or manipulative.

THE DIFFERENCE BETWEEN
INFLUENCE AND MANIPULATION

Have you ever watched a movie trailer and thought, *I've got to see that*? Or you watched a friend train for a 5K and downloaded a couch-to-5K app? Have you checked out restaurant reviews to figure out where to eat? Each are instances of influence—where someone has impacted your thoughts and decisions. When you're influenced, you choose to do something based off information from others.

When I worked in corporate, I had just started a new job when Ingrid marched up to my desk. With the false enthusiasm of a used car salesman, she effusively described a great opportunity she had for me. She wanted me to plan a retreat for the team. I sat quietly as she performed the acting role of her life. She told an elaborate narrative about how this would make my career and elevate my visibility.

No one wanted to plan the retreat and she thought she'd pass it off to the new person. I didn't have a problem being assigned the responsibility, but I did with her disingenuous and manipulative approach. She didn't care about my career or visibility—she no longer wanted responsibility for the work. She concocted an elaborate, insincere narrative and quickly made it on my list of people never to trust.

Influence involves choice. Manipulation often includes control of information, choice, perception, or even power. When people are being manipulated, something is being withheld. Information is presented in a calculated or made-up way. Authenticity is removed. There is often recognition of the intent to control the outcome instead of influence it. Many people have a keen sense of when they're being manipulated. They detect the false charm, misinformation, gaslighting, targeting of insecurities, and sometimes even sense a physical discomfort around the manipulating person.

Where Does Storytelling End and Propaganda Begin?

Stories that persuade share a point of view toward an intended outcome. Propaganda intentionally misleads, omits, or manipulates information to control an outcome.

Context Matters

Charities often tell the story of an individual, leaning into the emotion of their challenges. These stories are gripping, and your emotions are engaged.

I can't watch commercials for the American Society for the Prevention and Cruelty to Animals (ASPCA). It's too hard to watch the camera panning over trembling kittens with eye infections and malnourished puppies in cages while a sad ballad plays. While those commercials lean hard into emotions and discomfort, they're also clear about their intent: to raise awareness and money to prevent cruelty to animals and help them find loving homes.

Manipulation sets in when you aren't transparent about the information, intent, or context. Social media is an example of something that can be both influencing and manipulative. You may be influenced in your choices around food, travel, fitness, or books from social media posts. You're also manipulated by carefully constructed and edited images. You think you're looking at a real location or person, not realizing it doesn't look or exist that way in real life.

Empathy and Manipulation Aren't the Same Thing

A well-told story helps you empathize and relate with the characters. You develop an understanding of them or the situation they face, even if you fall into the out-group. It isn't manipulative to tell a story that engages the emotions of the audience. You want your stories to do that. Manipulation is experienced when information is intentionally added or withheld to change the narrative to create a specific outcome.

Think of something you have a strong belief in—like climate change. When you hear someone share an opposing view, you may be naturally skeptical as your brain tries to make sense of the information. *Are they sharing a well-thought-out idea? Do I trust them or this information? Is there an ulterior motive?* The more charged we feel, the more mental protests there often are to navigate.

Just because someone is working from a different set of beliefs and data doesn't mean they're being manipulative. Trust plays a big role in how we perceive information. Remember, oxytocin sends us a silent signal that we trust someone. We're more comfortable around them and generally open to what they say. Feeling stressed or defensive can inhibit this production of oxytocin. The more charged up the audience, the more work necessary to establish trust.

There isn't one formula for telling a story that helps people be open to different perspectives. The more heated the topic, the greater the likelihood that one story won't do all the work. It may take multiple stories and conversations over time to build empathy, trust, and understanding of each other.

The good news is that stories can create an opening, a common understanding, and a place to start a conversation and invite perspective. Even when people disagree. The key is to clearly communicate the intent and desired outcome of the story. Remember, your audience has a keen sense for detecting manipulative stories. The moment they feel attempts at manipulation, trust is lost.

WHAT IS YOUR RESPONSIBILITY AS A STORYTELLER?

Lead with intent. Be clear with your intent and perspective in your story. Particularly ones about a sensitive topic or with varying beliefs. By the end of the story, we should know why you're telling it and what you want the audience to know, think, do, or feel. The story can serve as a starting point to ask others their perspective.

When you tell a story that involves data, be transparent and explain the scope of the data. Address anticipated questions, objections, and what is still being explored. Don't just paint a positive picture; describe the challenges. Use the story to invite dialogue.

An HR team I worked with had a dashboard of data that was reviewed quarterly. They would tell the story of a few individuals within the data set to bring meaning to the data and then would zoom out to discuss the data at the company level. Their intent was clear: level set on the understanding of the data to support a thoughtful discussion. Had they only shared the stories of a few individuals and not fostered a broader discussion, their approach could have been seen as manipulative. By combining the stories and data at scale with discussions, they were able to have rich and nuanced conversations that wouldn't have otherwise resulted.

Don't try to manipulate emotions. For an event, I was once asked to create a story that would make people cry. That request made *me* want to cry. Can I tell you stories that would make you cry? Sure, we all can. But that doesn't mean we should. There is a difference between people authentically tearing up in response to a story that engages emotions and a story that one intentionally sets out to make them cry. Naturally connecting to emotions is key in storytelling. But do so in service of the desired outcome.

Treat people like adults. Not every setting needs a story. Don't use storytelling for policies, mandates, or dressing-up decisions. Especially around employee perks or benefits. If you're asking someone to do something they don't want to do, be straight with them. Don't colorfully describe all the reasons you think they will benefit. This lands as manipulative and insincere. At best, a skeptical eyebrow is raised and more likely, trust is eroded.

Stories create common understanding. Stories can provide context for an idea, perspective, choice, or set of data. Use the story to create a common understanding of the information as a starting point. Then ask people to share different perspectives.

The storytelling model is intended to help you create stories that result in increased trust from your audience. Be clear about your intent and transparent about your desired outcomes. The trust of your audience will flow.

Storytelling involves many steps, from finding and crafting the story to how you tell it. It's natural to feel vulnerable. In the next chapter, we explore how to navigate and embrace that vulnerability.

SUMMARY

When Does Storytelling Become Manipulative?

- There is a difference between telling a story for a desired outcome and telling a controlled narrative intended to mislead.
- Influence involves choice. Manipulation involves control. Information, choices, perceptions, and power are often distorted.
- Context matters in stories. Stories have transparent intent. Propaganda or manipulated messages distort the intent to support their narrative.
- A story that leans into your emotions and creates empathy isn't manipulative provided the intent is clear.
- Don't use stories to dress up situations where people should be treated like adults. Policies, mandates, or requirements shouldn't be disguised with a story.

EIGHTEEN

Vulnerability and Storytelling

Have you ever had a dream about giving a speech and couldn't remember a single word? Frantically, you tried to think, but your mind was as blank as a canvas without paint.

I blanked on the TED stage, and it wasn't a dream. It was awful and, oddly, unexpectedly wonderful. This was a few years before I gave the talk that is on TED.com. I was beta testing a MasterClass app that TED was developing for corporations. Testers were invited to their HQ in New York City to provide feedback.

One week before the event, I was chosen as one of three beta testers to give a talk on the TED stage in front of an audience. Most TED Talks are practiced for over six months. I had one week to prepare. I practiced my talk everywhere: in my car, backyard, in front of colleagues, at the gym, and even in the New York Public Library.

On the day of the talk, my nerves grew as I waited for my timeslot. Conversations happened around me, but all I could think about was taking the stage. I had no chill. I regularly give keynotes, but this one was higher stakes: the TED stage! When my name was announced, I took my place on the red circle. As the audience laughed at my opening story, I settled into the talk.

I was rounding the corner into the last quarter of my talk when it happened. My mind went blank. I didn't panic. But two seconds became five and then ten, and I realized I had no idea what to say. This was *not* how I envisioned the talk going.

TED Talks don't have a secret monitor with notes for speakers. An audience of faces stared, patiently waiting for me to resume. The only thing I could remember was what improv recommends when you blank: look someone in the eye to prompt your brain. One of my friends was sitting in the second row. I looked her in the eye and . . . nothing. I turned to my right and looked a stranger in the eye and . . . nothing. At this point, thirty seconds have passed. I could feel the audience growing uncomfortable for me.

I then thought of the second improv rule for blanking: fall on the floor. I start eyeing the red carpet under my feet thinking I might need to fake a fall. The audience began applauding with encouragement. My brain woke up and said, *"Oh no, we aren't done yet!"* I remembered the next sentence and finished my talk strong.

The whole day I had been counting down to go onstage. Now, I was counting the seconds until I could get off the stage! I felt I had ruined the whole talk by blanking. The whole point was to build an idea for the audience, and I hadn't done that.

Stephanie, a TED employee, approached me and said, "I really liked your talk." I thought she was just being nice, so I rolled my eyes. She continued: "I did. You recovered so strong. Much better than other people when they blank."

A week later, I was scrolling through LinkedIn and saw a post from someone who had attended the event but whom I hadn't met. His post included a quote from my talk. I was stunned. When the talk ended, I was certain it had flopped. Now, a week later, a stranger was quoting what I said. I began to think I'd built an idea after all.

Two months later, I was back at TED HQ to provide feedback in a different workshop. Another participant had been at my talk and repeated a different quote from it, describing how she had used the idea over the past few months.

A few hours later, during a tour of the TED offices, the guide said, "Here is where our talks are edited."

"Wait, are the talks often edited?" I asked.

"Oh sure, it happens all the time" she replied. "People often start sections over. Or they forget what they're going to say. Some walk offstage to find their place and then resume. We're human, it's no big deal. Those pieces are edited out for time and flow."

This is when I processed what Stephanie said to me after the talk—that I recovered better than others usually do. People blank on the TED stage all the time. We just don't realize it because we see edited talks.

I realized this story I was telling myself about the talk wasn't true. Sure, I had blanked, but my audience supported me. They didn't view it as a flaw. It made me authentic. They wanted me to succeed. Blanking didn't take away from ideas being built; it lent to them.

Blanking on that stage was such a rewarding lesson. I realized the audience is on your side cheering for you. Moments of vulnerability get the greatest response. Success isn't perfection. It's connecting through moments of authenticity.

Two years later, when I got the invite from Purdue to give my TEDx Talk, I approached it differently. I spent months preparing. My goal was to have fun building an idea for the audience. I wasn't afraid of blanking or making a mistake. That already happened, and I was fine! I knew to lean into the vulnerability in the moment and be authentic. As I finished the talk, I stood on the stage for a few seconds. It was a full-circle moment that never would have happened if I hadn't blanked on the stage years before.

NAVIGATING THE VULNERABILITY

Storytelling is vulnerable. There's no way around it. You often are communicating outside your comfort zone. It feels more personal than talking to slides or data—as if you're opening yourself up to judgment. It's natural to fear your audience may not like you or the idea you'll share. Your brain signals that you're doing something risky by increasing your heart rate and releasing cortisol and adrenaline. Everything feels heightened.

Dr. Andrew Huberman is a neuroscientist and professor at Stanford. He describes our physical response to something we dread as the same as those when we are excited. The difference is in the context and meaning we apply to our feelings. The only thing preventing an anxious moment from feeling exciting is our mindset. So, when you begin to feel anxious about an upcoming talk or presentation, focus instead on the excitement for building the best idea and story for your audience.

Who Are You OK with Disappointing?

Ed and I were standing in a room full of people where he was about to speak. He was the head of talent development for a company in the UK. We had spent weeks working together to prepare for this moment. He kept fidgeting with his collar, his belt, his hair—discomfort radiated off him. I asked him what he was feeling, and he said, "I'm afraid they won't like my stories or my presentation."

"Ed, if you were going to have me over to your home for dinner, what dish would you cook," I asked?

"That's easy, bangers and mash," he replied.

"OK, what are the odds that everyone in this room would like your bangers and mash?"

"Not very likely."

"Of course not. Some might be vegetarian. Some may find it too salty. Others may think it isn't salty enough. Would you take offense?"

"No, everyone has different preferences. I wouldn't take it personally."

"Exactly! Let's apply that same mindset to this situation. Focus on giving the best talk for those who will like it."

You aren't for everyone, and your story won't be either. There are already people who don't like you or something you've done. That's OK! You've made it this far in life with that being true. Because there are also people who love and want to hear from you. We each have different preferences and interests. If you try to make your stories meaningful and likable for everyone, they won't appeal to anyone.

Each time you communicate or tell a story, the most freeing question you can ask yourself is, *Who am I OK with disappointing?* Your story isn't for everyone, so don't focus on who won't like it. You can spin yourself several different ways trying to anticipate what may resonate. It's wasted energy, especially when they aren't your target audience.

The storytelling methodology begins with the audience for this reason. Focus on who you're talking to so you can tell them an appealing story. The persona and desired outcomes help you gain clarity about your audience. They also quiet the noise for those who aren't the intended recipient of your message. Even if they're seated in the same audience.

Don't Focus on the Outliers

As you prepare your story, you may find yourself focusing on the skeptics and outliers in the audience. It's natural since they're often the loudest voices. But your goal isn't to tell the story to the outliers or edges of your audience. Focus on the majority.

Outliers often need different stories and follow-up conversations to sway thinking. Something that's much easier after they've already seen the broader audience response to a message. It makes them think, *What am I missing? I see this differently,* and opens the door for a conversation. If your goal is to communicate solely with the skeptics, then plan a separate conversation.

The Story That Flops

There will come a time when you try to tell a story and it falls flat. It happens to each of us. It's a part of the process. You can work the storytelling process and tell a great story, and it can still fall flat. Your audience may be tired, hungry, or working through a personal challenge. The room temperature may be too hot or cold. The sound system or media may break. You can only control how you prepare, not how each story lands.

While these moments can feel uncomfortable, most of the discomfort sits in your head. Your audience isn't expecting perfection. When you tell stories that don't resonate, they think, *Eh, that's not for me* or *I don't like that story,* and they move on. The trick is for you to do the same.

Ever seen a comedian tell a joke that doesn't work? They acknowledge it and keep moving. Sometimes they even poke fun at themselves. They don't dwell on it. The joke that crushes at the 7 p.m. show may flop at the 10 p.m. show. It doesn't mean it's bad. It wasn't the right fit for that moment. Or the audience was hungry. Your appreciation for a comic doesn't falter because you don't like one of their jokes. Those jokes are forgotten. You remember the ones that resonate for you. Same with your stories.

Not all your stories will land as clearly as you picture them in your head. If a story falls flat, acknowledge it and move on. Most of the time, you can see why it didn't work. Learn what you would do differently, and don't hold onto the experience.

The Vulnerability Sunburn

There is a physical side to vulnerability. It's a bit like a sunburn. When you spend a day in the sun, your skin radiates warmth for several hours after. Each time you move, you flinch as your clothes rub the sensitive skin, reminding you of the sun exposure.

When you tell a story, you radiate vulnerability. You may even flinch as you replay the story in your mind. This is the result of putting yourself out there and feeling exposed. You can experience this whether your story is a smashing success or a terrible flop. Much of it happens as your neurochemicals rebalance to your normal levels.

| When you tell a story, you radiate vulnerability. |

No one thinks about you as much as you think of yourself in these moments. When I blanked my first time on the TED stage, I felt like there was a billboard with my photo and "She blanked onstage!" on it. Two months after the event, attendees didn't remember me blanking, but they did remember my ideas.

Watch how you talk to yourself in these moments. Don't create an elaborate narrative in your mind. Part of becoming a great storyteller is telling some stories that don't work. It's how you find the ones that do!

Embracing Vulnerability

We respond to vulnerability because it's authentic, relatable, and human. You don't have a great story without vulnerability. And you can be vulnerable without oversharing or telling private information.

Your vulnerability will be the thing to which your audience responds. Each time I work with a leader struggling to tell a story, I find a small opportunity for them to tell one. Because like it or not, you can't think your way through vulnerability. The only antidote is to tell a story. Motivation comes from action, not waiting to be inspired to act. Once these leaders experience the audience's reaction, they're open to telling stories again. The next time, they lean further into vulnerability.

> Motivation comes from action,
> not waiting to be inspired to act.

It can be unnerving to tell stories if those around you don't tell them too. Particularly at work. Role-model how storytelling can lead to different ways of communicating, understanding, and talking with each other. Help evolve the culture of communication in your company by showing how to tell an effective story. Even if others default to talking at people or sharing fifty slides of data. Don't tell them why storytelling is impactful; show them.

It Hasn't Been Told by You

My storytelling workshops often begin with the same activity: "Draw happy. Whatever you conceive that to be, draw it." Participants receive these simple instructions and are set forth to create. When we each look at each other's drawings, many have the same themes: families, vacations, or hobbies. Each is unique. I use this to reinforce the point that a story may have been told before, but not by you. Storytelling is personal. You bring your unique perspective and should tell the story only you can tell. We don't learn from encountering the same thing repeatedly—we learn from differences. Your stories provide perspectives that no one else shares in the same way.

Stories Earn You Permission to Tell More

The stakes for storytelling can feel high, as though there is one opportunity to tell a story. You rarely have one instance to tell a story. Telling stories earns you permission to tell more stories for your audience. And one story often won't do everything you'd like. Your audience may need different stories.

Companies that sell products and services need to tell multiple stories describing the various problems experienced by their diverse audience. Pain points, challenges, and how to solve them are tackled throughout different stories. It's these specific stories that create the *"I'll have what she is having"* feeling in their customers. Rarely will a company find one story that does all the work they need to influence and inspire action. They use specific stories for specific audiences to connect them to the desired outcome.

Your Audience Is Rooting for You

They want you to do well. Even when your story falls short of what you had hoped for, your audience isn't turned off. They want authenticity and relatability, not perfection.

The vulnerability that occurs when someone tells a story doesn't just belong to the storyteller; part of it also belongs to the audience. They're open to feeling something through your story, and it's up to you to take them there. Build on their energy. Use your personas to talk directly to individuals in your audience. Engage the senses. Create an immersive experience by building and releasing tension. Leverage the audience's curiosity. Pull them forward with ideas. Create a perfect balance of this push-and-pull energy to bring you both to a different place at the end of the story.

The Most Important Story Is the One You Tell Yourself

When I was eleven years old, my family was on vacation in Virginia. We stopped at the Busch Gardens amusement park in Williamsburg. They had a new rollercoaster called "The Big Bad Wolf." Instead of sitting in a car on the track, the seat was suspended below the track with your legs dangling. It took me several minutes to work up the courage to go on the ride. To this day, when it comes to riding rollercoasters, I idle somewhere between nervous and excited. In this case, my inner gauge tilted all the way over to nervousness. I grasped the handles so tightly that my fingers turned white.

The rollercoaster slowly pulled us up the ascent, making the clanging sound, like a timer ticking off seconds. My heart was beating in my throat. As we crested the top of the first drop, we hovered there long enough for me to think, *What am I doing?* The ride dipped forward, and I became weightless. Fear and anticipation were replaced with laughter. My inner gauge flung over to excitement for the rest of the ride. As we lurched to a halt at the end, I had one thought: *Let's go again.*

Telling stories is a bit like working up the courage to go on a rollercoaster. You feel nervous, and the anticipation begins to grow. As soon as you finish and see the reaction, you immediately want to do it again. That's the best way to start. Vulnerability isn't a reason to avoid telling a story—it's the reason *to* tell one. Experience the energy shift with your audience and the empathy and trust they gain for you. Notice how fun it can be.

The most precious thing an audience can share with you is their attention. Don't squander that by throwing information at them. Honor their attention by helping to inform, influence, or inspire through stories. Embrace vulnerability. Be the you-est version of you. Your audience will not only respond positively to your stories, but they'll also ask for more.

I still experience vulnerability when I tell stories. You will too. Instead of avoiding it, take it as a signal to lean in harder. The response and experience of telling a story are always worth it. Tell stories whether you feel scared, anxious, vulnerable, or excited. Trust your personal gauge will flip to excitement. Know that someone needs to hear your stories.

The most important story you'll ever tell is the one you tell yourself. Don't talk yourself out of telling stories before you start because they feel vulnerable. They haven't been told by you—and you have a unique and interesting perspective to share on this wild ride of life.

SUMMARY

Vulnerability and Storytelling

See the checklists in the back of the book.

- As you prepare your stories, ask yourself, *Who you are OK with disappointing?* Your story isn't intended for everyone. Free yourself by determining exactly who it's for and who you are OK not connecting with.
- You will tell stories that fall flat. If you don't, you aren't telling enough stories. When your story falls flat, acknowledge it, learn from it, and move on.
- Vulnerability has a physical component like a sunburn. You notice differences as your neurochemicals level out after telling a story. Be aware of this and plan for it. Be mindful of how you talk to yourself during this time.
- No one is in your head as much as you are.
- Stories may have been told before, but not by you. Your audience wants to hear your perspective.
- Your audience is rooting for you. They want you to tell fantastic stories and be moved by them.
- Movement, especially those involving forward motions, helps release dopamine. Put these in your stories to help move around energy.
- You can't think your way out of vulnerability, and motivation doesn't create action. Your action creates the motivation to tell stories.
- The most important story you'll tell is the one you will tell yourself.

PART FIVE

The Takeaway

Landing the Idea

A few years ago, I spent an afternoon on a beach outside of San Francisco. It was an overcast day, calling for a jacket instead of sunglasses. I had the entire beach to myself. Sitting on a big piece of driftwood, I listened to the waves hitting the sand, each one like a satisfying cymbal crash. My jacket flapped in the wind as I looked out toward the horizon. The grey sky met the dark, swirling, white-capped water. The Pacific Ocean was living up to its turbulent reputation that day.

I noticed a surfer in a black wetsuit paddling out to the wave line. He turned his board toward shore and immediately tried to catch a wave. I've never stood up on a surfboard, yet I could tell everything he was doing was wrong. He started paddling too late. When he popped up, he struggled with his balance. Instead of getting the feel for the wave, he immediately turned right and face-planted into the ocean.

He climbed back up on the board, laid on his stomach, and paddled back into position. His next three attempts were no different. His timing was off, and he couldn't catch his perfect wave.

I never said a word to the surfer, but I felt like I could hear his inner dialogue breaking down each step:

Paddle, paddle, paddle!

Pop up now!

Drop your shoulder.

Bend your knees. Turn right!

Wave after wave, I watched him try to stand. Each attempt ended the same way: face-planting in the ocean, the surfboard spiraling in the air and ocean water spraying upwards in a funnel before raining back down over him.

After seven attempts, he no longer tried to catch waves. He started drilling each step in the process. First, he worked on the timing of his paddle to catch the wave. Then he practiced popping up on the board at the right time. Next came mastering balance. I could see him working through the mental checklist of what he had been taught, fighting for every move. He got better with each piece he practiced, yet he still hadn't caught a wave.

After an hour, he sat on the board with his legs dangling on either side in the cold, marbling water. His weary shoulders were hunched over, and he was breathing hard. He looked rumpled on the surfboard. As the board rose and fell with the swell of each wave, he pinched his nose and wiped the water from his face. I sensed his inner dialogue debating if he should quit for the day. Something inside him said, *Give it one more chance.*

This time, everything was different. He had internalized each step and was in a state of flow. His body was free from stiffness and tension. He started paddling at the right time. The pop-up was perfect. There was an ease to his movement and maneuvering of the board. Instead of turning right, he deftly turned left. He caught his perfect wave and rode it back to the beach. As his board hit the sand, he picked it up and carried it to his car with a big smile on his face.

He figured out how to apply each of the steps in a way that felt genuine to him. Instead of fighting the board, he moved with it. He took everything he learned and leaned into his instincts. He didn't force the perfect wave; he put together all the pieces to catch it.

Just as the surfer was in search of his perfect wave, you're in search of the perfect story each time you tell one. You want each story to land the idea for your audience by connecting them to the takeaway. This is what makes the story perfect—it informs, influences, or inspires your audience toward the outcome you desire for them.

The storytelling model walks through the steps to find and tell the perfect story for each audience. The Five Factory Settings of the Brain help your audience feel immersed, as though they're the Walt and Maria of your stories. They connect the audience to the emotions you want them to feel. Their brains spend calories on the stories, making them engaging and memorable. Like surfing, storytelling is a compounding skill. The more you do it, the better you get. As you internalize the process and the steps, you'll find your authentic style for telling the perfect story.

You can learn to be a great storyteller. Follow the steps of the model and the Five Factory Settings to put the pieces together for each audience. The most valuable thing people can do is give us their attention. Great stories respect that attention by thoughtfully building an idea that informs, influences, or inspires the audience.

You don't have to wait for the perfect idea, situation, or invitation to tell stories. The only requirement is deciding to try. Stories create connections, open doors, and leave people changed. Someone out there needs to hear your stories. The only thing missing is that you haven't told them yet.

Don't wait for the perfect story. Take your stories and make them perfect.

Checklists

Test Story

Create Audience Persona & Define Outcomes

Make Everything Earn Its Place

Collect & Select Potential Story Ideas (ongoing)

Build Story Structure

Apply Five Factory Settings

Add Details, Engage Senses & Emotions

Sequence the Story

DEFINE YOUR STORYTELLING APPROACH CHECKLIST

- **How do you find your best ideas for stories?**
  - ☐ Ask yourself a question and go for a walk.
  - ☐ Interview other people.
  - ☐ Seek out conversations.
  - ☐ Dig into client testimonials or feedback.
  - ☐ Review questions that commonly come from clients/customers.
  - ☐ Look at pictures (on your phone, online searches, stock photo websites).
  - ☐ Search online.
  - ☐ Visit experiences in the world (museums, movies, performances).
  - ☐ Find articles, books, podcasts.
  - ☐ Talk with a muse.
  - ☐ Other: _____

- **Where will you capture potential story ideas?**
  - ☐ Notebook
  - ☐ Online tool/app
  - ☐ Spreadsheet
  - ☐ Post-its
  - ☐ Other: _____

- **When you build out a story, do you:**
  - ☐ Discuss it with someone?
  - ☐ Start with an outline?
  - ☐ Write it out in its entirety?
  - ☐ Create a bulleted list of key points?
  - ☐ Say it aloud and record it?
  - ☐ Use visual aids to support your story?

STORYTELLING PROMPTS CHECKLIST

- **Personal Experiences**
  - ☐ What was a defining event in your life?
  - ☐ What was a situation that didn't start funny, but you laugh about it now?
  - ☐ What would do differently if you could?
  - ☐ When did you have an adventure on vacation?
  - ☐ What pets did you have growing up?
  - ☐ Do you have a hidden talent?
  - ☐ Who was your favorite teacher?
  - ☐ What was your first concert, car, or date?
  - ☐ Have you had a car breakdown? What did you learn?
  - ☐ What would you save if your home was on fire?
  - ☐ What is the best advice you've received?
  - ☐ What is a skill or talent you mastered?
  - ☐ What traditions were observed in your home?
  - ☐ What is something you should have thrown out but can't part with?
  - ☐ Ask a friend or family member:
    - What is your favorite thing about me?
    - What was I like as a child?
    - What did you imagine I would do for a living?

- **Professional Experiences**
  - ☐ What was your first job?
  - ☐ What was a mistake or failure you learned from?
  - ☐ What was a difficult team or project you experienced?
  - ☐ What change made you afraid of losing or gaining something?
  - ☐ Who was your best or worst leader?
  - ☐ What is a moment where you thought, *This is why I do this work!*
  - ☐ When was a moment when you had no idea what you were doing?
  - ☐ What is something you would like to do over?
  - ☐ What would you tell the younger version of yourself?
  - ☐ What are you most proud of?
  - ☐ What is the best advice you have received?

- **Clients, Customers, Stakeholders**
  - ☐ What problems do your customers face? What do they complain about?
  - ☐ What do your clients aspire to be, do, or have in the future?
  - ☐ What are the pain points you have solved for your customers?
  - ☐ What do customers love about your product or solution? Why?
  - ☐ What do your customers think of you?
  - ☐ Which of your customers' challenges would you find if you searched online sites? (search engines, stock photo sites, social media)
  - ☐ What have you learned from the evolution of your product or solution?
  - ☐ What are the ten principles or ideas your customers need to know?
  - ☐ Why did you launch a particular product or service?

■ **Find a Muse**

- ☐ What would make someone your ideal customer?
- ☐ What problems do they struggle with?
- ☐ How have you helped them, and what did they realize in the process?
- ☐ Where have they had success?
- ☐ What comes easily to them?
- ☐ Where are they looking to grow?
- ☐ What aspirations do they have?

■ **In the World**

- ☐ What is a favorite movie or piece of art that moves you? Why?
- ☐ What music (an artist, song, or genre) can you play endlessly?
- ☐ What topics can you talk about all day?
- ☐ What is an outdoor space you love to visit?
- ☐ Have you ever heard the origin of a product/company that stuck with you?
- ☐ Do you have a favorite museum?
- ☐ Is there an article or podcast episode that stood out to you? Why?
- ☐ What is your favorite city or place to visit? Why?
- ☐ Do you have a favorite book?
- ☐ Have you heard a speech or speaker that stayed with you?

■ **Passage of Time**

- ☐ Is there a conference room or building that's witnessed different meetings or events over the years?
- ☐ Did you have a stuffed animal, blanket, or piece of clothing that followed you on multiple experiences?
- ☐ What are objects that have evolved over the passage and time (e.g., rotary phone, cordless phone, flip phone, mobile phone)?
- ☐ Is there any object that has been passed down through your family?
- ☐ What are different world events your audience has witnessed over their lifetime?
- ☐ What is an object that could tell multiple points of experience? For example, my hiking boots are twenty-five years old. They represent many stories of the different hikes, trips to different countries, and life events.

- **Eulogies**
  - ☐ What do you admire about this person?
  - ☐ When did the person do something that was "so them"?
  - ☐ What is your favorite thing about this person?
  - ☐ What is the funniest situation you saw this person in?
  - ☐ If you could relive a day with this person, what would it be?
  - ☐ What is a story about this person that no one knows?
  - ☐ What was this person particular about—like food not touching on a plate?
  - ☐ How did you meet this person?
  - ☐ What holidays, vacations, or experiences did you share with the person?
  - ☐ What's a funny quirk about this person, like *always* taking a photo with a finger in the frame?

- **Wedding Toasts**
  - ☐ When did you meet the couple?
  - ☐ What have you learned from the couple?
  - ☐ What was the behind-the-scenes story of their engagement that most guests wouldn't know?
  - ☐ What is your first memory of them individually or as a couple?
  - ☐ How have you seen them grow as a couple?
  - ☐ When did you know they were meant to be?
  - ☐ What is an example that demonstrates who they are as a couple?
  - ☐ Do you have a specific theme for the toast like "love" or "longevity"? If so, what is a story about the couple that embodies the theme?

Job Interviews

- **Prepare for the interview**
  - ☐ What do you know about the interviewer?
  - ☐ What do you want the interviewer to know about you?
  - ☐ Why are you the right one for the role (in-group)?
  - ☐ What do you uniquely bring to this role or organization (out-group)?
  - ☐ What assumptions might the interviewer have about you?

- **Tell me about a time . . . story prompts**
  - ☐ Tell me about a time you faced conflict with a co-worker or team.
  - ☐ Describe a time you made a mistake.
  - ☐ Give an example of a time you demonstrated leadership skills.
  - ☐ What is an example of when you had to reset expectations with a client?
  - ☐ When did you have to think on your feet?
  - ☐ Share a problem you have solved.
  - ☐ How have you navigated a challenge?

Job Interview Story Structure

- **Challenge or conflict:** What was the problem or conflict you addressed? What was at stake? Why was this messy or hard? What would've happened if nothing had been done?
- **Outcome:** What action did you take?
- **Result:** What was the result of your actions?
- **Learning:** What did you learn?

STORYTELLING CHECKLIST

- **Define the persona(s) for your audience:**
  - ☐ What brings this group of people together to be your audience?
  - ☐ What do they have in common?
  - ☐ What is the average age of your audience?
  - ☐ What is the education experience of your audience?
  - ☐ What type of role or expertise do they hold?
  - ☐ Where does your audience live?
  - ☐ What hobbies does your audience participate in?
  - ☐ What does a typical day look like for them?

- **What is the opportunity to tell a story?**
  - ☐ What do you want your audience to know, think, do, or feel differently?
  - ☐ What idea or question will you explore with your audience?
  - ☐ Do you want to bring your audience to experience discomfort, aspiration, or joy?
  - ☐ Who are you OK disappointing with this story that isn't your target audience?

- **What is your goal in telling this story?**
  - ☐ Entertain.
  - ☐ Inform/educate.
  - ☐ Challenge or expand thinking.
  - ☐ Influence, inspire, or motivate.

- **Picking an idea for a story to tell:**
  - ☐ Which idea builds what you want the audience to know, think, do, or feel differently?
  - ☐ Does the idea create discomfort (seeing things that can't be unseen) or pleasure/aspiration (things we want to be, do, or have)?
  - ☐ Does the idea help the audience feel part of or different from the group?

- ☐ Can you combine two ideas or compare one with the future?
- ☐ Does the idea change if told from a different perspective?
- ☐ Which of these are you excited to tell?

- **Four-part storytelling model—write out a sentence for each:**
  - ☐ *What is the context?* What is happening, why should the audience care?
  - ☐ *What is the conflict?* What is the moment where something happens? What is the fuel for the story?
  - ☐ *What is the outcome?* What is the result of the action taken?
  - ☐ *What is the takeaway?* What is the overall theme and message?

- **Make characters relatable:**
  - ☐ What are the names of the major characters?
  - ☐ What is important for the audience to know about their age or physical description?
  - ☐ What should the audience know about the personality of your characters?
  - ☐ Why are the characters in the story?
  - ☐ What conflict do the characters face? Is it with themselves or with others due to circumstances, actions, or desires?
  - ☐ How is conflict reconciled throughout the story?
  - ☐ What are the emotions of the characters throughout the story? Do their emotions change throughout the conflict?
  - ☐ How do the characters evolve across the story? How are they changed by the end?

- **Details and senses:**
  - ☐ What is the time and place of the story?
  - ☐ How can you anchor details to what the audience already knows?
  - ☐ Are there metaphors or comparisons you can incorporate?
  - ☐ What are at least three specific details, like eating chocolate-chip ice cream.

☐ Engage at least two senses: help us see, hear, feel, taste, and smell what is happening.

☐ Show us what the characters are feeling.

- **What is the best flow for your story?**
  ☐ *Linear*: beginning, middle, and end.

  ☐ *Flashbacks*: linear stories that pause and share a flashback that sets context before continuing.

  ☐ *Circular*: start and end at the same place (often "Conflict").

  ☐ *Start at the end*: start at the end and go through the context and conflict.

  ☐ *Parallel story*: multiple stories sharing people, plots, or themes in common.

  ☐ *Change perspective*: stories told from the perspective of different characters.

  ☐ *Compare, Contrast, Imagine if* . . . : visioning or strategy sessions.

  ☐ What is the best perspective to tell your story from?

  ☐ How will you start your story?
  - Start with a question.
  - Start with a statement about the theme of the story.
  - Jump into the conflict.
  - Use the unexpected.
  - Appeal to curiosity.

- **Leverage the Five Factory Settings**
  ☐ *Build and release tension*: include unexpected phrases, details, events, or order to minimize the lazy brain and assumptions.

  ☐ *Senses*: engage at least two senses.

  ☐ *Details*: include at least three specific details.

  ☐ *Emotions*: show the emotions the characters experience.

  ☐ *Library of files*: connect details and events to what people already know.

  ☐ *Relatable characters*: Do we understand why they do what they do even if we don't agree with their actions? What changes do they undergo?

□ *Pleasure/pain*: Does your story intentionally make the group uncomfortable or inspired?

□ *In-/Out-group*: Does your story help the audience feel a part of a group or idea—or intentionally not part of it?

□ *Pithy phrases*: Can you make the takeaway succinct?

■ **Make everything earn its place and test your story:**

□ Does this move the story forward?

□ Does this engage the senses?

□ If it was cut, what would be lost?

□ Does this create confusion?

□ Does something need clarification?

□ Does anything need to be added or removed?

□ Can common phrases or details be replaced with specific ones?

□ Where is the energy high in the story?

□ Where does the energy dip?

□ If you change the order of the story, does it impact the energy?

■ **Preparing to tell your story:**

□ What is your opening sentence?

□ What are your transition sentences?

□ What is your closing sentence?

□ What gestures can you use in your opening sentences?

□ What gestures can you use to evoke emotions?

□ When will you accelerate and/or slow down your cadence and inflection?

□ Where will you pause around your key points to land ideas?

□ Where else will you use pause in the story?

□ Where do you want the energy high?

□ Where do you plan to bring the energy down for a bit?

□ Prepare your mindset:

  • Focus on building an idea for your audience.

  • Take on the excitement of a child wanting to show you something.

  • Tell yourself, "Have a conversation."

STORYTELLING WITH DATA CHECKLIST

- **What is your opportunity to tell a story with data?**
  - ☐ Create mindset shifts, openness for exploration, and connect to deeper understanding.
  - ☐ Level set new audience or stakeholders on history, current status, and future focus.
  - ☐ Key decisions or milestones.
  - ☐ Inform insights about data (trends, outliers, unexpected results, further exploration).
  - ☐ Demonstrate scale.

- **What is the problem you are trying to solve?**
  - ☐ Ideally define this before collecting data. What problem are you trying to address, explore, or decide with the data? Frame this as a question.

- **What decision is needed?**
  - ☐ One time decision: *What is happening?*
  - ☐ Ongoing monitoring of trends and identifying outliers: *Why are things happening?*
  - ☐ Forward-looking, predictive, or informing strategy: *What might happen in the future? What should we consider next?*

- **Define your audience:**
  - ☐ What is their current understanding of the problem statement?
  - ☐ What is one thing you want them to know, think, feel, or do as a result of the data?
  - ☐ What are potential obstacles?

- **What is your recommendation about the data?**
  - ☐ What do you learn as you analyze the data?
  - ☐ What insights does the data provide?
  - ☐ What is important to know about the data?

☐ What is surprising or unexpected about the data?

☐ What do you recommend?

☐ Are you informing a decision or discussion?

☐ Define specific questions for the discussion or decision, if different from your problem statement.

■ **Identify the smallest amount of data:**

☐ What is the smallest piece of data you can share to inform your problem statement and recommendation?

☐ Within that data:

• What problems are faced?

• What pain points are experienced?

• What happens if something is or isn't done?

■ **Find a story for the data:**

☐ *Tell a story about the data*: Tell a story about the smallest piece of data (e.g., person, team, organization).

☐ *Tell a parallel story*: What is an idea that aligns with the takeaway you want your audience to know, think, do, or feel differently? What stories can connect to the overall theme and outcome you want for the audience?

■ **Building the data story:**

☐ *What is the context*: What is the problem statement you set out to solve?

☐ *What is the conflict*: What are you seeing in the data? What is unexpected or surprising?

☐ *What is the outcome*: What is the impact? How does the data inform the problem statement?

☐ *What is the takeaway*: What is the recommendation? What happens if nothing is done?

■ **Data visualization:**

☐ Show one thought per slide/page.

- ☐ Don't rely on charts or graphs to tell the story. Pull the idea out of them. Use infographics.
- ☐ Use headers to guide the story and insights. Put supporting content in an appendix for reference.

Acknowledgments

Thank you to the fans of storytelling and TED Talks. This book is an illustration of what can happen when you have an idea worth spreading. To current and future storytellers, I look forward to you finding your stories and making them perfect.

Thank you to Matt Baugher and Andrea Fleck-Nisbet for helping to make this book a reality. Thanks to Amy Kerr for the copy edits and to Austin Ross for helping refine my vision for making storytelling accessible. Thanks to Jeff Kleinman for providing early thoughts and enthusiasm. Roger Freet, thank you for immediately seeing and advocating for the value of this book and reminding me to be of good cheer.

Many people played a role in the various steps leading to this book in your hand. From inviting me to speak at Purdue and TEDxPurdueU, offering support in the book proposal, informing stories, connecting me to interviews, or reading drafts. Thank you to: Roti Balogun, Walt Bettinger, Mhorag Doig, Lindsay Eberts, Samantha Hartley, Nancy Hunt, Kelly Lafnitzegger, Cathy Leonard, Alberto Lopez de Biñaspre, Richard MacLagan, Kayla Nalven, Katie Lynn Sears, Megan Prince, The TEDxPurdueU team, Maria Rogers, Laura Grace Sears, Petra Schultz, Jeff Tetz, Kristen Vesey, and Erin Willis. Thank you to Ellen Singer for helping instill my love of writing.

Thank you to each of my clients for informing my stories and to my Brain Food newsletter community for the questions and discussions that inspired many points in this book.

A group of individuals graciously said yes to storytelling interviews well before there was a book. Thank you to: Chris Brogan, Heather Davidson, Laura Elliott, Josh Fleming, Chelsea Hardaway, Rebecca Koegel, Kathy Klotz-Guest, Sean Murray, Kathleen O'Connor, Pam Sherman, Caitlin Weaver, and Samantha Zarinni.

I am so grateful to each storyteller for sharing wisdom in their interview vignettes. Thank you to: Will Csaklos, John Cushing, Drew Dudley, Peggy Fogelman, Serena Huang, Sarah Austin Jenness, Michelle Satter, Evan Skolnick, Stephanie Stuckey, Gary Ware, Colby Webb, Anthony Williams, Bofta Yimam, Paul Zak, and Manoush Zomorodi.

Kathleen O'Connor, thank you for sharing your book writing process and encouraging me to write my own. John Wisdom, thank you for generously sharing your wisdom and encouragement while somehow predicting all of this. Ellen Gundlach, thank you for the soft serve and the invitation that triggered this chain of events. Darren Raymond, thank you for reading each iteration of this book and always knowing the right words to say at the right moment. Cheri Shannon, thank you for test reading and giving the perfect nudge, support, and encouragement. Sara Ley, thank you for saying yes to that pilot and pushing me forward—who would've thought? Susan Harrow, I am forever grateful to you for playing such a significant role in making this book a reality.

To my aunts, uncle, and cousins: Thank you for wonderful moments that have informed my thinking and stories over the years. To my in-laws, thank you for welcoming me into your family full of stories and curiosity.

To Kris, Dave, Dean, and Madison, we hold a lifetime of stories together; and lucky for you, my memory is long. Thank you for all the experiences, love, laughter, and adventures together. To many more!

To my parents: thank you for instilling my love of reading, writing, and storytelling. You've given me all the ingredients to make the perfect story. Thank you for sharing your love and encouragement every step of the way.

Ron, thank you for creating the artwork in the book and patiently helping with my random questions. Thank you for your love, unconditional support, and encouragement. And for not asking "Why?" when I said we were going to see the Oscar Mayer Wienermobile—but instead asking "When?"

References

INTRODUCTION: DON'T EAT THE CRAYONS

Karen Eber, "How your brain responds to stories–and why they're crucial for leaders," PurdueU TEDx Talk, February 2020, https://www.ted.com/talks /karen_eber_how_your_brain_responds_to_stories_and_why_they_re _crucial_for_leaders.

Adam Bryant, "Walt Bettinger of Charles Schwab: You've Got to Open Up to Move Up," *New York Times*, February 4, 2016, https://www.nytimes.com/2016/02 /07/business/walt-bettinger-of-charles-schwab-youve-got-to-open-up-to-move -up.html.

ONE: STORYTELLING TO THE RESCUE

Kathy Caprino, "Former NASA Director Shares Leadership Lessons from Catastrophic Spaceflight Disasters," *Forbes*, November 10, 2017, https://www.forbes.com/sites /kathycaprino/2017/11/10/%EF%BB%BFformer-nasa-director-shares-leadership -lessons-from-catastrophic-spaceflight-disasters/?sh=3f4ce8a56f1c.

Paul J. Zak, "Why Your Brain Loves Good Storytelling," *Harvard Business Review*, October 28, 2014, https://hbr.org/2014/10/why-your-brain-loves-good-storytelling.

"What We Know Now: How Psychological Science Has Changed Over a Quarter Century," Association for Psychological Science, October 31, 2013, https://www .psychologicalscience.org/observer/what-we-know-now-how-psychological-science -has-changed-over-a-quarter-century.

Jerome Bruner, *Actual Minds, Possible Worlds* (Boston: Harvard University Press, 1987).

Sarah Austin Jenness, interview with the author, August 16, 2022.

TWO: WHAT HAPPENS WHEN
YOU TELL STORIES?

Marcus E. Raichle and Debra A. Gusnard, "Appraising the brain's energy budget," *Proceedings of the National Academy of Sciences of the United States of America* 99, no. 16 (August 2002), https://www.ncbi.nlm.nih.gov/pmc/articles/PMC124895/.

Dr. Lisa Feldman Barrett, "How emotions trick your brain," *BBC Science Focus*, May 2018, https://www.sciencefocus.com/the-human-body/how-emotions-trick -your-brain-2/.

Dr. Lisa Feldman Barrett, "That Is Not How Your Brain Works," *Nautilus*, December 18, 2021, https://nautil.us/that-is-not-how-your-brain-works-2-13339/.

Stephanie A. Sarkis, Ph.D., "Why We Hate Not Finishing What We Start: . . . and a possible route to greater satisfaction," *Psychology Today*, March 31, 2014, https://www.psychologytoday.com/us/blog/here-there-and-everywhere/201403 /why-we-hate-not-finishing-what-we-start.

Dr. Lisa Feldman Barrett, "There's more than one way to carve up a human brain," *BBC Science Focus*, January 22, 2022, https://www.sciencefocus.com/the-human -body/brain-regions/.

Pragya Agarwal, "What Neuroimaging Can Tell Us about Our Unconscious Biases," *Scientific American*, April 12, 2020, https://blogs.scientificamerican.com /observations/what-neuroimaging-can-tell-us-about-our-unconscious-biases/.

Roger E. Bohn and James Short, "How Much Information? 2009 Report on American Consumers," University of California, San Diego, January, 2009, https://www .researchgate.net/publication/242562463_How_Much_Information_2009 _Report_on_American_Consumers.

Kayt Sukel, "Beyond Emotion: Understanding the Amygdala's Role in Memory," Dana Foundation, March 13, 2018, https://dana.org/article/beyond-emotion -understanding-the-amygdalas-role-in-memory/.

Ashley Hamer, "Here's Why Smells Trigger Vivid Memories," *Discovery*, August 1, 2019, https://www.discovery.com/science/Why-Smells-Trigger-Such-Vivid -Memories.

Doug Ramsey, *"UC San Diego Experts Calculate How Much Information Americans Consume,"* December 9, 2009, http://calit2.net/newsroom/release.php?id=1630.

Linda C. Lin, Yang Qu, Eva H. Telzer, "Intergroup social influence on emotional processing in the brain," *Proceedings of the National Academy of Sciences of the United States of America* 115, no. 42, (October 2018), https://www.ncbi.nlm .nih.gov/pmc/articles/PMC6196546/.

Jessica Martino, Jennifer Pegg, and Elizabeth Pegg Frates, MD, "The Connection Prescription: Using the Power of Social Interactions and the Deep Desire for Connectedness to Empower Health and Wellness," *American Journal of Lifestyle Medicine* 11, no. 6 (October 2015), https://www.ncbi.nlm.nih.gov/pmc/articles /PMC6125010/.

Paul J. Zak, "The Neuroscience of Trust," *Harvard Business Review*, January–February 2017, https://hbr.org/2017/01/the-neuroscience-of-trust.

Jonny Thomson, "Why are some people more curious than others?" *Big Think*, December 31, 2021, https://bigthink.com/neuropsych/curiosity-in-humans/.

Olivia Guy-Evans, "Broca's Area Function and Location," *Simple Psychology*, June 28, 2021, https://www.simplypsychology.org/broca-area.html.

Jaap M. J. Murre and Joeri Dros, "Replication and Analysis of Ebbinghaus' Forgetting Curve," *Plos One Journal*, July 6, 2015, https://doi.org/10.1371 /journal.pone.0120644.

JAWS, directed by Steven Spielberg (1975; Universal City, CA: Universal Pictures), film.

John Lennon, "Imagine," *Imagine*, Apple Records, 1971.

Greg J. Stephens, Lauren J. Silbert, and Uri Hasson, "Speaker-listener neural coupling underlies successful communication," *Proceedings of the National Academy of Sciences of the United States of America* 107, no. 32 (July 2010), https://www.pnas .org/doi/10.1073/pnas.1008662107.

Pauline Pérez et al, "Conscious processing of narrative stimuli synchronizes heart rate between individuals," *Cell Reports* 36, no. 11 (September 2021), https://www.cell .com/cell-reports/fulltext/S2211-1247(21)01139-6?_returnURL.

Michelle Satter, interview with the author, July 7, 2022.

THREE: CREATING DESIRED OUTCOMES

"Budweiser: Puppy Love," directed by Jake Scott, aired January–February 2014, https://www.imdb.com/title/tt8290392/.

Paul Zak, Ph.D., "Why Inspiring Stories Make Us React: The Neuroscience of Narrative," *Cerebrum: National Library of Medicine* (February 2015), https://www.ncbi.nlm.nih.gov/pmc/articles/PMC4445577/.

Paul J. Zak, "How Stories Change the Brain," *Greater Good Magazine*, December 17, 2013, https://greatergood.berkeley.edu/article/item/how_stories_change_brain.

Paul Zak, "Trust, morality—and oxytocin?" TED Global, filmed July 2011, https:// www.ted.com/talks/paul_zak_trust_morality_and_oxytocin?language=en.

REFERENCES

Antonio Damasio, *Descartes' Error: Emotion, Reason, and the Human Brain* (New York: Vintage Books, 2006).

Ferris Jabr, "Why Your Brain Needs Downtime," *Scientific American*, October 15, 2013, https://www.scientificamerican.com/article/mental-downtime/.

Marcus E. Raichle and Mark A. Mintun, "Brain Work and Brain Imaging," *Annual Review of Neuroscience* 29, no. 449–476 (July 2006), https://www.annualreviews.org/doi/abs/10.1146/annurev.neuro.29.051605.112819.

Gardiner Morse, "Decisions and Desire," *Harvard Business Review*, January 2006, https://hbr.org/2006/01/decisions-and-desire.

Chun Siong Soon et al, "Unconscious determinants of free decisions in the human brain," *Nature Neuroscience*, April 13th, 2008, https://www.nature.com/articles/nn.2112.

Max-Planck-Gesellschaft, "Decision-making May Be Surprisingly Unconscious Activity," *Science Daily*, April 15, 2008, https://www.sciencedaily.com/releases/2008/04/080414145705.htm.

A R Damasio, "The somatic marker hypothesis and possible functions of the prefrontal cortex," *Philosophical Transactions of the Royal Society of London* 29, no. 351 (October 1996), https://pubmed.ncbi.nlm.nih.gov/8941953/.

Jason Pontin, "The Importance of Feelings," *MIT Technology Review*, June 17, 2014, https://www.technologyreview.com/2014/06/17/172310/the-importance-of-feelings/.

Adam Piore, "This Is How Our Brain Makes Decisions," *Discover Magazine*, June 12, 2017, https://www.discovermagazine.com/mind/this-is-how-our-brains-make-decisions.

Rae Ann Fera, "The 'Story Button' in Your Brain: Neuroscience Study Sheds Light on Brand/Human Love," *Fast Company*, March 12, 2014, https://www.fastcompany.com/3027563/the-story-button-in-your-brain-neuroscience-study-sheds-light-on-brand-human-love.

Paul Zak, Ph.D., "Why Inspiring Stories Make Us React: The Neuroscience of Narrative," *Cerebrum: National Library of Medicine* (February 2015), https://www.ncbi.nlm.nih.gov/pmc/articles/PMC4445577/.

Joe Lazauskas, "This Tiny Neurotracker Could Change the Way Brands Measure Engagement," *Fast Company*, March 10, 2018, https://www.fastcompany.com/40542354/this-tiny-neurotracker-could-change-the-way-brands-measure-engagement.

Jeff Beer, "Exclusive: Your brain is lying to you about Super Bowl ads. This neuroscientist can prove it," *Fast Company*, February 1, 2019, https://www.fastcompany.com/90300169/your-brain-is-lying-to-you-about-super-bowl-ads-this-neuroscientist-can-prove-it.

Immersion, https://www.getimmersion.com/v4/why-it-works.

Paul J. Zak, "How to Run a Con," *Psychology Today*, November 13, 2009, https://www
.psychologytoday.com/us/blog/the-moral-molecule/200811/how-run-con.

Dr. Paul Zak, interview with the author, June 1, 2022.

FOUR: CREATE AN ENDLESS TOOLKIT OF POTENTIAL STORY IDEAS

Marcus E. Raichle and Mark A. Mintun, "Brain Work and Brain Imaging," *Annual
Review of Neuroscience* 29, no. 449–476 (July 2006), https://www.annualreviews
.org/doi/abs/10.1146/annurev.neuro.29.051605.112819.

"Peek Under the Hood," Oscar Mayer, https://omwienermobile.com/peekunderthehood
.html.

Gary Ware, interview with the author, June 10, 2022.

FIVE: START WITH YOUR AUDIENCE, NOT WITH THE STORY

Bofta Yimam, interview with the author, June 28, 2021, August 9, 2022.

SIX: SELECT AN IDEA FOR YOUR STORY

Roger Fisher and William Ury, *Getting to Yes: Negotiating Agreement Without Giving
In,* (New York: Penguin Publishing Group, 2011).

"2020 Custodians Are Key Winner", Tennant, July 29, 2020, https://www.tennantco
.com/en_ca/blog/2020/07/2020-custodians-are-key-winner.html.

Stephanie Stuckey, interview with the author, August 15, 2022.

SEVEN: DO I HAVE TO TELL A PERSONAL STORY?

Drew Dudley, "Everyday Leadership" TEDxToronto, filmed 2010, https://www.ted
.com/talks/drew_dudley_everyday_leadership.

Drew Dudley, interview with the author, May 27, 2022.

EIGHT: OUTLINE YOUR STORY STRUCTURE

"Writing 101: What is The Hero's Journey?" Masterclass, September 3, 2021, https://www.masterclass.com/articles/writing-101-what-is-the-heros-journey.

Kenn Adams, "Back to the Story Spine," *Aerogramme Writer's Studio*, June 5, 2013, https://www.aerogrammestudio.com/2013/06/05/back-to-the-story-spine/.

Star Wars, Episode IV - A New Hope, directed by George Lucas (1977; San Francisco: Lucasfilm Ltd.), film.

Manoush Zomorodi, interview with the author, July 6, 2022.

NINE: ADDING DETAILS THAT MATTER

Kainaz Amaria, Jen Kirby, and Jennifer Williams, "The Devastating Notre Dame Cathedral Fire, in 19 Photos," *Vox*, April 15, 2019, https://www.vox.com /world/2019/4/15/18311852/notre-dame-cathedral-fire-spire-collapse-photos -pictures-paris-france.

Will Csaklos, interview with the author, June 21, 2022.

TEN: MAKE US FEEL SOMETHING

Jaws, directed by Steven Spielberg (1975; Universal City, CA: Universal Pictures), film.

Spielberg, directed by Susan Lacy, aired 2017 on HBO Max, https://www.hbomax .com/feature/urn:hbo:feature:GWZc7Pgn3NcJ7wgEAAAAJ.

Esther Havens and Taylor Walling, "Meet Jean Bosco," Charity: Water, https://archive.charitywater.org/stories/meet-jean-bosco/.

Susan Richard, "Shelter Pooch Turned Poster Dog: Say Hello to Dan," CBS New York, August 22, 2015, https://www.cbsnews.com/newyork/news/shelter-pooch -turned-poster-dog-say-hello-to-dan/.

Colby Webb, interview with the author, May 29, 2020, June 14, 2022.

ELEVEN: SEQUENCE YOUR STORY

Good Will Hunting, directed by Gus Van Sant, written by Ben Affleck and Matt Damon (1997; Los Angeles: Miramax), film.

Rives, "The Museum of Four in The Morning," TED Talk , filmed 2014, https://www.ted.com/talks/rives_the_museum_of_four_in_the_morning.
Evan Skolnick, interview with the author, June 14, 2022.

TWELVE: MAKE EVERYTHING COUNT

La La Land, directed by Damien Chazelle (2016; Santa Monica; Lionsgate), film.
Malorie Cunningham, "The making of 'La La Land': Why it's important to modern cinema," ABC News, February 21, 2017, https://abcnews.go.com/Entertainment /making-la-la-land-important-modern-cinema/story?id=45112391.
"Culture Eats Strategy for Breakfast," Quote Investigator.com, May 23, 2017, https://quoteinvestigator.com/2017/05/23/culture-eats/.
Peggy Fogelman, interview with the author, July 22, 2022.

THIRTEEN: STORYTELLING WITH DATA

Terry Reith, "Passengers angry and frustrated as cruises ship renovations ruin vacation," Canadian Broadcasting Corporation, April 3, 2018, https://www .cbc.ca/news/canada/edmonton/norwegian-cruise-passengers-angry-1.4603237.
Enjoli Francis and Matt German, *"Bucket list' cruise ruined by construction work, Norwegian Sun passengers say,"* ABC News, April 6, 2018, https://abcnews.go.com /US/bucket-list-cruise-ruined-construction-work-norwegian-sun/story?id=54295211.
Adam Piore, "This Is How Our Brain Makes Decisions," *Discover Magazine*, June 12, 2017, https://www.discovermagazine.com/mind/this-is-how-our-brains-make-decisions.
Serena Huang, Ph.D., interview with the author, August 17, 2020, June 25, 2022.

FOURTEEN: TELLING YOUR STORIES

Brandon Stanton, Humans of New York, https://www.humansofnewyork.com/.
Lindsey D. Salay, Nao Ishiko, Andrew D. Huberman, "A midline thalamic circuit determines reactions to visual threat," *Nature* 557, no. 183–189 (May 2018), https://www.nature.com/articles/s41586-018-0078-2.
John Cushing, interview with the author, June 3, 2020, July 18, 2020.

FIFTEEN: HOW DO I KNOW IF MY STORY RESONATES?

Dr. Anthony Williams, interview with the author, August 1, 2022.

SIXTEEN: WHERE DO STORIES GO WRONG?

Gabriella Paiella, "Instead of a Fearless Girl, We Could Have Had a Fearless Cow," *The Cut*, June 7, 2017, https://www.thecut.com/2017/06/fearless-girl-statue -wall-street-was-almost-a-cow-statue.html.

Linda Massarella, "'Fearless Girl' was originally supposed to be a bronze cow," *New York Post*, June 7, 2017, https://nypost.com/2017/06/07/fearless-girl-was-originally -supposed-to-be-a-bronze-cow/.

Karen Eber, "Make Waffles, Not Spaghetti," January 2018, https://www.kareneber .com/blog/wafflesnotspaghetti.

SEVENTEEN: WHEN DOES A STORY BECOME MANIPULATIVE?

Ruchi Sinha, "Are you being influenced or manipulated?" *Harvard Business Review Ascend*, January 26, 2022, https://hbr.org/2022/01/are-you-being-influenced -or-manipulated.

Stephanie Strom, *"Ad Featuring Singer Broves Bonanza for the A.S.P.C.A.,"* New York *Times*, December 25, 2008, https://www.nytimes.com/2008/12/26/us/26charity .html.

EIGHTEEN: VULNERABILITY AND STORYTELLING

TED MasterClass, https://masterclass.ted.com/.

Matt Abrahams and Andrew Huberman, "Hacking Your Speaking Anxiety: How Lessons from Neuroscience Can Help You Communicate Confidently," Stanford Graduate School of Business, May 14, 2021, https://www.gsb.stanford.edu /insights/hacking-your-speaking-anxiety-how-lessons-neuroscience-can-help -you-communicate.

About the Author

Karen Eber is an international consultant, keynote, and TED speaker. As the CEO and Chief Storyteller of Eber Leadership Group, Karen helps Fortune 500 companies build leaders, teams, and cultures one story at a time.

Her clients include ADP, Big Four Consulting Firms, Carrier, Facebook, General Electric, Kraft Heinz, Microsoft, Kate Spade, Stuart Weitzman, MIT, London School of Business, and Stanford University. She is a four-time American Training and Development winner and frequent contributor to publications, including *Fast Company*.

Karen has more than twenty years of experience and has been a Head of Culture, Chief Learning Officer, and Head of Leadership Development at General Electric and Deloitte. Karen lives in Atlanta, Georgia, plays the flute and piccolo, goes on *carpe diem* runs, and prefers waffles to spaghetti.

For more information about Karen Eber,
visit www.kareneber.com

Book Karen Eber as a keynote speaker:
https://www.kareneber.com/speaking

Inquire about a Storytelling Workshop or Coaching for your company:
info@kareneber.com or https://www.kareneber.com/storytelling

Join Karen's *Brain Food* newsletter:
https://www.kareneber.com/brain-food